To John Myers

ELEMENTS OF INFORMATION MANAGEMENT

by
Blaise Cronin
and
Elisabeth Davenport

The Scarecrow Press, Inc.
Metuchen, N.J., & London
1991

British Library Cataloguing-in-Publication data available

Library of Congress Cataloging-in-Publication Data

Cronin, Blaise.
    Elements of information management / by Blaise Cronin and
Elisabeth Davenport.
      p. cm.
    Includes index.
    ISBN 0-8108-2406-X
    1. Information resources management. I. Davenport, Elisabeth.
II. Title.
T58.64.C76   1991   91-14512
658.4'038—dc20

CONTENTS

1
MODELS, METAPHORS AND METONYMS

Formal Models

Why do we think the time is ripe for another text on information management? There are several reasons: we are acutely conscious of the limitations implied by previous definitions; we wish to explore the management implications of a technology base which can offer immense flexibility and transformative power; and we want to draw attention to infrastructural developments which have outpaced traditional mechanisms for control of information.

The term information management is commonly associated with formal representation of information entities and flows to facilitate the construction of computer models which allow specific functions (transaction processing, decision making, information retrieval) to be automated. Exactness and objectivity are central to this approach, which is based on the manipulation of symbols, mathematical description and the search for appropriate algorithms. In terms of system design, however, processes which are consistent and complete may distort the reality which the system is intended to represent where underlying models fail to take account of fluctuations, unforeseen events, and human affect.

It might be said that formalists "lose the place," by constructing mechanisms for prediction and control which are complete in themselves, but difficult to implement in context. We invoke, as others have done, a simplistic model from cognitive science to both illustrate and explain the problem: a mechanistic and reductionist perspective relies heavily on the left hemisphere of the brain [see exhibit 1.1] which controls our numerical and analytic capabilities. The excesses of such an approach to management can be balanced by cultivation of output from the right side of the brain (which controls affect, affinity, perception of pattern).

Managers must search for analogies as well as analyze; explore affect as much as efficiency, and recognize the relevance of context. There is a growing emphasis on soft systems modeling, organic decision making, construct mapping and the craft of strategy.[1] You cannot teach people

EXHIBIT 1.1

Process of the Left and Right Hemispheres

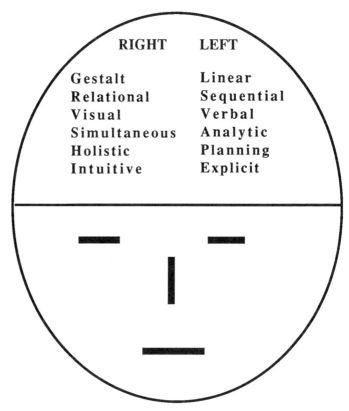

intuition, but you can help them trust their own judgment, by making them aware of how it has been formed, and of the biases and prejudices which are brought into play. And, of course, you can make them aware of these processes in others.

By emphasizing metaphor (describing one thing in terms of another) as a primary modeling component of information management, we offer an alternative to the formalist approach, one which allows managers to understand and exploit affinities. The affinity may be between things (you see your network as a traffic system); it may also be between people and things (if information is a weapon, you will want combative resource managers).

Shifting Paradigms

A good manager will develop a feel for what is appropriate in terms of models and modeling techniques. In our view, information scientists and system designers are not synonymous with information managers. The former use models to test and lay bare the conceptual foundations of the field, or to devise systems which perform consistently and with the requisite level of functionality. An information manager, however, exploits information to satisfy specific organizational objectives: to get from here to there, in other words. The models used are pragmatic instruments of change.

What do we mean when we suggest that a model may be an instrument of change? By taking a new perspective, by adopting a new metaphor, managers may more successfully align resources with new objectives. The concept of paradigm shifts may serve as an illustration.[2] It takes a visionary to break a paradigm, to make new observations or interpret existing data differently. A classic case is plate tectonic theory, for which Wegener was derided in the first decades of the century, to be vindicated in the '60s when magnetic scanning of the sea bed confirmed his hypothesis. Wegener's theory was comprehensive and integrative; it pulled together many phenomena with one explanation, but it was not testable (and thereby acceptable) until an adequate technology base emerged.

We believe that perspective changes and paradigm shifts are part of the stuff of management, and that managers should be encouraged to make them. The good manager will spot which paradigm is *passé* because of developments in technology or ideology; s/he will identify emergent agents and instruments and their potential impacts. Paradigms may even be acquired off-the-shelf, as it were: Porter's work has transformed perceptions of the value of information *and* information technology by stressing the strategic significance of connectivity and linkages within and between companies. We discuss his value chain concept in detail in chapter 3.

We hope that our book will take managers beyond formalism; we also hope that it will take them beyond the data processing, information systems, library or records management department of their organizations. Information managers can be found across a range of industrial sectors and line functions, handling information at different levels of aggregation, from the byte to the information center. Our primary interest, as academics and consultants, is in information management at the perceptual and conceptual level, in information as it is perceived by the senses, heard, read, written, seen, keyboarded and spoken. For others, information management, more accurately information engineering, is defined in terms of the sub-atomic realm of bits, bytes and code.

Everday Information Managers

In a sense, all of us are information managers: many of the information typologies, systems and exchanges which characterize our domestic interactions are small-time versions of their professional counterparts (though where our domestic technological base is inadequate we contract out our processing to third parties: banks, insurance agencies). Everyday life entails management of a number of physical commodities: you manage the contents of the larder, your domestic fuel, your wardrobe, usually by placing items in usage-related sets: food which decays quickly is placed in the freezer, bottles and cans go in the cupboard. Apart from managing our domestic economy, we also manage the body's internal economy, with bouts of energy followed by periods of relaxation, or calorie ingestion followed by a *régime minceur*. Such processes are monitored and modeled by taking one's pulse, or stepping on the scales. Intangibles like time, or credit, are also managed at the personal level, modeled with the help of calendars, personal organizers, investment plans and bank statements. The simple 2 × 2 matrix in exhibit 1.2 is an illustration.

EXHIBIT 1.2
Personal Asset Management Matrix

	TANGIBLE	INTANGIBLE
INTERNAL	Bodily organs	Energy
EXTERNAL	Food Property	Credit Time

You act as an information manager when you store, file and refer to the records which constitute your civic and legal personalities (national insurance numbers, medical cards, certificates of birth, marriage and death, mortgage documents, title deeds). What you keep, how long you keep it, how you classify it, will depend on a range of factors, and these will change according to prevailing circumstances. When you buy a car, you may remove your licence from your set of statutory documents, and relocate it with insurance policies, purchase agreements, guarantees, as it makes more practical sense to include it in the document set for "you as car driver and owner" than "you as licensed citizen." For most of us, classification is relative.

We all manage intimate information at the personal level which is trapped on paper, on tape, on video, in photographs. These materials may be filed in chronological order, as they attach to significant events, according to context. Such holdings may contain official and unofficial documentation; sometimes the two are merged in a record of an occasion: a wedding for example, trapped in its album, certificate of marriage primly adjacent to the wedding breakfast menu.

Informal Information

There is also a mass of less structured information, phone calls, ephemera, conversations, which is rarely managed in the way we have just defined, except in the underworld of sleuths and paid informers or gatherers of intelligence, who trap such information, classify and interpret it without the subject's knowledge. What is for most of us simply the stuff of social interaction is, for these people, an asset, a resource or, in the case of blackmail, a weapon.

Personal information embraces the formal and informal; the structured and unstructured. It can also be seen in terms of spatial analogy or spheres of influence: domestic, street, terrain and horizon. Domestic information, which may be

EXHIBIT 1.3
An Information Typology

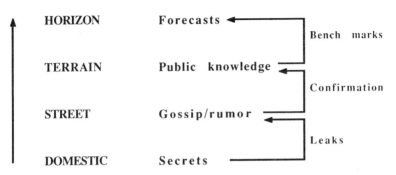

secret or proprietary, is contained within the source environment (the family or company), but can seep out into the wider world as rumor or speculation. Street information of this kind is exchanged in real-time, lacks structure and tends to be disseminated by gossips and industry insiders, through invisible colleges, and old boy networks. As speculation hardens and leaks are confirmed, the process of refinement and consolidation begins, resulting in a corpus of more or less structured terrain information, from which it is possible to make projections and forecasts about future events, what we[3] term horizon information [see exhibit 1.3].

This typology or model is a grappling hook for unstructured, unofficial and intimate information at the level of the organization, where such material has hitherto been no more amenable to control than in the personal arena.

Codes of Conduct

Informal communication, whether in the domestic setting or workplace, may lack structure, but it is regulated by tacit codes and etiquettes (the norms of scientific behavior posited by Merton[4], but observable in other contexts) which bond us into groups, clans, clubs, families, intimates. Often these voluntary ties are stronger, more binding, than those imposed by formal contracts, a phenomenon crystallized in the concept of *confianza*. This type of information is a driving force in any society, from the level of the small workgroup to the multidivisional corporation. It can be trapped and exploited in great detail. The technology exists, and ranges from crude phone tapping (phone calls are tape recorded to prevent breaches of Chinese walls in finance houses) to the application of hypermedia systems, but the ethical and ethological effects may be ambivalent.

Total transparency may not always be a virtue, at work or play: there may be good reasons to hide dirty linen, strategic agendas and *liaisons dangereuses,* and that is why a conventional structure of reporting and recording has emerged: the protocols which structure meetings and their minutes, and the coded, edited, summarized or otherwise sanitized formats which mask accountability in many organizations. The plenary picture derived from total monitoring of an organization's or individual's information activities is bound to differ from, and may even conflict with, the summary representation or model, which is used in public presentation and negotiation (official communiqués, press releases, annual reports, party political broadcasts, display advertising).

Total Intelligence Management

Though many reporting structures and protocols have honorable origins (the reduction of opacity by the introduction of due process), they can outlive their usefulness and themselves become agents of opacity, which obstruct the identification of uniquely significant events. You cannot see the trees for the wood.

This is, of course, a restatement of the problems raised by formalism: selection and standardization may increase transparency and consistency, but they may exclude significant phenomena. Technologies exist which can overcome the problem, by accommodating the teeming detail of an information universe (in distributed storage) while allowing appropriate abstractions to have their day and be replaced as their context changes. Total intelligence has emerged from the military closet (like many developments in the information field) and put on its pin-stripe suit. The legal and regulatory implications of this demobilization have not begun to be addressed. We conclude our introduction with a quotation from Brand, whose long-sighted information prospectus is one of the few texts to raise major issues: "The structure of the world information economy is being determined by traffic rather than policy in part because there's no world body politic, in part because there's no workable theory of what's happening."[5]

From Modeling to Managing

What are the conditions of information management? How can something intangible, inexhaustible, immensurable be analyzed and bounded? How can something with such properties be harnessed, controlled and exploited? In what sense can information be managed?

Information can be managed because it can be modeled. That is the starting premise of this book. Three types of model are important in information management. Metaphorical models which describe one thing (the target) in terms of another (the source); metonymic models where the part of something stands for the whole. This may result in a reduced, stylized or summary representation or version of the thing described: a planetarium showing the workings of the solar system, a label on a bottle of wine giving vintage, alcoholic strength, appellation, grower, shipper; an abstract of a technical article presenting the methodology and main conclusions, a flow chart describing a standard set of procedures, keywords used as surrogates to characterize the contents of a document.

Our third type of model is a set or taxonomy, like a classification scheme, thesaurus or Venn diagram, which binds or relates discrete entities on the basis of apparent elements in common. By helping us describe entities and events, and the relationships and linkages between them, models help us understand the surrounding world.

Metaphorically Speaking

Modeling in this broad sense is fundamental to cognition and communication, the primary information activities. It may be unobtrusive, where metaphors are used reflexively and implicitly to shape our perspective: we *waste* time . . . we *invest* effort . . . we *die* of boredom. Lakoff has explored the implications of describing time as a resource: "If I live in a society that is constructed on the TIME IS A RESOURCE metaphor, and if I accept and function in terms of that metaphor, then it can be *true* that *someone wasted an hour of my time this morning.* This makes sense on an experientialist account of truth; it makes very little sense on an objectivist account of truth."[6]

Our daily discourse is replete with such usages. When we speak of information as a resource we activate a train of associations (prospecting, identifying, extracting, refining, exploiting) which may influence the way it is viewed and handled in a particular context. Such casual usage may in fact be the foundation of a methodology, when the basic metaphor is developed into a sustained analogy, with multiple correspondences between source and target. Horton's approach to information mapping[7] is a case in point, where an organization's information resources and entities are identified and literally mapped [see exhibit 1.4].

Our three types of model, metaphor, metonymy, and classification, impose structure on what is alien, protean and slippery, and they can range in detail from simulators, through full-blown design specifications, to flow charts and matrices, to single words, keywords, or distinctive metaphors.

EXHIBIT 1.4

Information Mapping

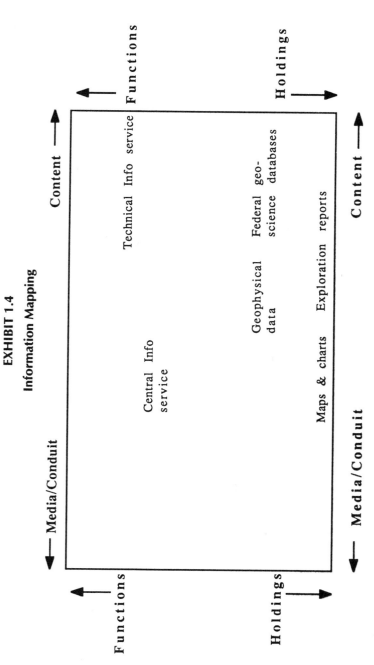

Each of the three broad classes is rooted in usage. We classify so that we can exploit what is classified more efficiently. We summarize so that relevance may be rapidly apparent. We use metaphors to describe and prescribe. They work in two ways; as homing devices implicitly guiding us in our engagement with the unfamiliar, or as lenses which allow us to exploit the familiar in unfamiliar ways. In exhibit 1.5 we present a number of commonly used metaphors, ranging from resource to commodity, along with a variety of metonymic and classificatory approaches.

Information has distinct properties which make it difficult to manage, but we would suggest that these can be overcome by looking at other areas to find analogous situations where processes and properties have been modeled to achieve definable results. The term model is used here in the most generalist way, embracing metaphor, and in the next section we tease out some examples. These have been chosen from colloquial, largely metaphorical, accounts of information handling and from the mainstream management literature. Exhibit 1.6 offers a selection of sources, from chemistry to property, and the related models/metaphors. This approach is highly eclectic and care must be taken to distinguish between literal and figurative usage. In some cases, the relationship between source and target is extremely delicate, and the two may be confused.

EXHIBIT 1.5

METAPHOR	METONOMY	CLASSIFICATION
Resource	Icons	Hierarchic
Weapon	Keywords	Synthetic
Property	Abstracts	Semantic nets
Asset	Summaries	Graph theoretic
Commodity	Screen menus	Clumping

EXHIBIT 1.6

SOURCE DOMAIN	METAPHOR / MODEL
CHEMISTRY	Elements, properties, processes, laws
PHYSICS	Power generation/transmission, opto-electronics, entropy
LIFE SCIENCES	Morbidity, mortality, genetics, epidemiology
EARTH SCIENCES	Seismology, plate tectonics
ECONOMICS	Input-output, econometrics
MANAGEMENT SCIENCE	Traffic systems, norms/standards
PROPERTY	Intellectual property rights, information broking, information futures
WARFARE	Battle management systems, intelligence gathering, strategy
MANUFACTURING	Warehousing, distribution, marketing, packaging
PSYCHOLOGY	Cognitive processing, neurology, linguistics, organizational behavior, bonding, semiotics

To illustrate the benefits of the metaphorical approach, and how the new can be grasped with the help of the familiar, we look at the world of applied science, across a range of disciplines. For us, this has proved a useful source domain.

Metaphors We Manage By

What do applied science and information management have in common? Both involve a search for explanation, and thus control, which entails deconstruction, analysis and reconstruction. Entities and processes are described in terms of models, and tested across a range of contexts.

These can be broken down, evaluated and classified for a particular purpose. The systems architect may choose bits as the basic building blocks; a chief information officer may configure his resources in terms of megablocks of data, equipment and personnel. The behavior of these quasi elements may be observed under controlled conditions; where regular patterns appear, and where these are consistent across a range of circumstances, they achieve the status of laws. Where the building blocks are words or documents, the classic laws of information science apply, based on the observation of statistical regularities in the production and consumption of information.[8]

In the database context the building blocks may be fields: the information contained on an employee record, for example, written in ordinary prose, is broken down into elements such as age, sex, experience, skills, which are recombined in a relational database to achieve more rapid and effective transaction processing. What you choose to define as the elements in any such process will vary with level of aggregation: you can operate at the level of the bit, pixel, word, node, frame, field, record, tuple, document, file, database and ultimately at the level of the hardware and human resource configurations which constitute operational systems.

Chemistry

To many non-scientists, chemistry is the archetypal applied science. It involves elements, properties, processes, reactions, controlled conditions (heat, pressure, time), the analysis and breakdown of substances (through oxidation and reduction, for example) and their recombination to produce a desired output. Just as chemical elements have specific properties (valency; atomic weights; combustibility) information elements have properties: 1 or 0 (at the level of the bit); meaning, position and frequency (of terms); length (of word/numeric strings); number, format and degrees of standardization (of fields, frames, records and files); flatness or relationality (of files and databases). Exhibit 1.7 contains a selection of information elements with their corresponding properties and associated processes.

Control of environmental conditions (response to heat, pressure and time) is an essential component of the management of chemical reactions, and is the basis of classic laws like those of Boyle or Lavoisier. The laboratory conditions which embody such control are an integral part of popular conceptions of science.

These have their equivalents in information management. You can tweak or fine-tune a model to throw more information from more sources at a problem. For instance, you can broaden or narrow a search statement which restricts or amplifies output (improved precision versus improved recall); or you can reduce or accelerate the speed at which information flows (by changing the baud rate or limiting password access). Pressure to provide information is manifest in a range of situations, from the extreme case of interrogation to the hothouse environment of a Wall Street dealing room. Time dominates many information transactions: the month-end report is a classic example. Because periodic transaction reporting is easy to control, many organizations mistakenly believe that this function *is* information management and neglect material which falls outside this purview, what we earlier called "street" information.

Crisis management, whether of natural disasters or the breakdown of a laser printer, requires ad hoc and urgent information. How do you manage the insidious, the unex-

EXHIBIT 1.7

ELEMENTS	PROPERTIES	PROCESS
Bit	1 and 0	Combination
Word	Meaning Position Frequency	String Interpretation Selection Combination
Pixel	Resolution	Combination
Node	Link to/from	Switching
Frame	Consistency	Matching
File	Flat/relational Multi-user	Searching Merging Inverting
Book	Discrete package Portability Serial access	Storage Lending
Network	Local/wide Multi-user Multi-functional	Sharing Linking Transporting
Library	Multi-user Organisation	Storage Collection Dissemination Archival
Expertise	Embodied Scarce Expensive	Knowledge- engineering Consultation

pected, the highly specific, the highly volatile? Trace elements (the insidious components of chemical compounds) are identified and controlled with improved instrumentation (for sensing, monitoring and calibration; the flame test is superseded by electrospectroscopy). The same applies in the management of rogue information, where improved instrumentation in advanced storage, matching and retrieval technologies supports executive decision making.

In chemical experiments conditions are manipulated to test outcomes. Simulation and scenario spinning are analogues in information management where the variables might be market share, unit costs, ROI (return on investment), or product substitution, data on which are fed into an executive information system (EIS), and the results matched against subsequent business performance.

Light and Energy

Like information, energy is intangible, yet we have no problem in understanding what is meant by energy management. Think of electricity. At the simplest level it is created by the conversion of kinetic energy, from the motion of a turbine, into electrical current which in turn is converted into heat, kinesis or whatever. Controlled generation is possible because regularities exist in the behavior of electrons in magnetic fields, and these are described in the laws of electromagnetism.

Just what are the analogies with the generation of information? On the basis of anecdotal evidence at least, there appears to be higher creativity where there is more information flow, just as faster flow through turbines generates more power. But the similarities are difficult to sustain. Electrical charge is a carrier of information in the controlled environment of the integrated circuit, which complicates discussion of analogues in this area. To talk of transmission in this context is to describe the actual flow (source *becomes* target).

Power generation and transmission, however, have their metaphorical uses, and these are well-established. These processes may be managed by large public utilities with distribution over a national grid or privately at the enterprise level where an organization has independent generating facilities. Most people access information through public utilities (networks of libraries, advice bureaux, government agencies), but those who have special requirements (for exclusive or timely information), or whose work is information-intensive, may bypass public services and their concomitant limitations to use private utilities (internally or externally sourced) where quality of service is assured.

Current must be transformed at different points in the transmission system in order to sustain flow from national grid to household; information must also be rendered compatible with different technologies if it is to flow across organizations or departments. Hence the importance of standards. The transformation of energy across different phases of the power production cycle can be compared with media transformations in information transfer: in both cases, the number of phase boundaries or transactions is inversely proportional to the efficiency of the process, with heat loss in the physical environment analogous to loss of precision in messaging.

The phrase "half-life" triggers off a train of association with nuclear fission. The decay of radionuclides is measured in terms of half-life and so is subject-related documentation (for the sake of argument, the half-life of quantum physics publications is six months, of economic history, ten years). One technique for identifying the benefits of investment in information technology is the value chain (see chapter 3), which aids understanding of the compound impact, or ripple effect, of information across organizations, an impact akin to a chain reaction in nuclear physics.

Light provides many metaphors for information handling: speeches are held to be illuminating, someone may be asked to throw a little light on the subject, presentations may be enlightening. Like electrical charge, photons are physical carriers of information in the context of laser and fiber optics. Like information, light can be described in terms of a duality of waves (flows in the case of information) and particles (information entities). Like light, information may be diffracted (in the form of rumors or whispers or *samizdat* circulation) by a barrier (embargoes, censorship, language, culture). It may also be refracted by different media: viscous prose slows down assimilation by obscuring or distorting meaning; graphics may facilitate absorption. There is a popular measure of such opacity, the Fog Index.

Information is sometimes described as negentropic, which means that it appears to counteract the universal tendency of all systems to decay into disorder. This paradox can be explained in terms of Shannon's law: he maintains that resolving power is an essential characteristic of information and relates the information attached to a message to the probability of transmission. In most messages there is a high degree of redundancy: common or less significant terms appear frequently. "Resolving power" describes those terms in a message which are distinguished by being more significant and thereby more useful than the rest. There are fewer of them, and they are less likely to be successfully transmitted than more mundane terms. In Shannon's theory entities with a low probability of getting through have a high information content.[9]

The concept of entropy has also been invoked to justify investment in information, as information is widely held to reduce uncertainty by structuring disparate quanta. In the world of business information, this concept appears as value added, where structure and formatting transform raw data (the second condition of information management). Where information is excessively duplicated and over-circulated, it loses its resolving power and confirms the law of entropic decay (sometimes invoked as the Second Law of Thermodynamics), as overload leads to confusion, paralysis or simply to disregard. Overload, per se, can also impair decision making.[10]

The Life Sciences

Models from the life sciences pervade the description of information behavior. These may relate to bodily functions (physiological models like the brain of the firm[11]) or behavioral patterns: models based on foraging (gathering, weeding, storing, cooking, distribution), cross-fertilization (bibliographic coupling; co-citation), the life cycle, mortality rates. Some models are bidirectional. Dawkins has based a book on information as the focal metaphor for life: "What lies at the heart of every living thing is not fire, not warm breath, not a 'spark of life.' It is information, words, instructions." He points up the similarities between DNA and computer memory: "DNA is ROM . . . All the DNA in each of ourselves is addressed in the same sense as computer ROM, or indeed computer tape, is addressed . . . there is a sense in which the collective data bank consisting of the ROMs of an entire species can be constructively written to. . . ."[12] The information technology of life is digital (the genome project is an attempt to establish the ultimate information bank); the construction of proteins is described in terms of transcription, communication and reading, all information activities.

A para-evolutionary folklore has emerged from the notion that information confers competitive advantage (we discuss this in chapter 3). Competition for niches is a driving force behind intelligence gathering; the fittest, those who survive, can be equated with the most informate. Information is essential to both predators and prey. New species arise from parent populations to exploit changing substrates in a turbulent physical environment, as companies renew or transform their efforts in volatile markets by altering scope, by product differentiation or through new pricing strategies. Transient niches mean rapid turnover of populations (witness the recent global growth in merger and acquisition activity); flexibility, or the ability to diversify, becomes the key to survival; cross breeding (joint ventures; mergers and acquisitions, to extend the parallel), a rejuvenation strategy.

Illness is a major source of metaphor for the malfunction of information systems: indigestion, bloat, bugs, viruses (in certain cases, spread by promiscuous sharing of software). Many of these are described in terms of the etiology of disease or epidemiology (contagion has often been used to model the diffusion of ideas), and the insights which emerge from such analysis are the basis of measures which are, in effect, preventive medicine (vaccines, screening, identification of high risk cases, or *cordons sanitaires* ranging from obscenity laws to closed user groups). The professional consultant and information counselor are the equivalent of physicians.

Psychology

Both cognitive and social psychology provide models to explain information behaviors and can improve systems design (think of neural networks, or the concept of cognitive authority as embodied in expert systems). Knowledge engineers, for example, seek to map and trap in an expert system the know-how and information skills of recognized experts. The extent to which such a system appears to model cognition will be a measure of its success. Attempts to model cognition in terms of mind-as-machine, or formal logic processes, are, however, proving difficult to sustain.

We think much of the time by association, with patterns of association reflecting our experiences of the real world. Yet, classic information retrieval systems are based on pattern matching of decontextualized terms which limits their usefulness. An inflexible metonymic paradigm (search by surrogate) can never hope to do justice to authorial meaning and intention. A cluster of new storage and publishing technologies with the generic label hypermedia offers an alternative to conventional statistical approaches to information retrieval. The user makes connections and links between dispersed and fragmentary information entities (documents, images, sounds) and thus the user, rather than the indexer, or another intermediary, decides what is significant.[13]

Perception theory and semiology help explain how information is received, sifted, processed, interpreted, retained and acted upon. The models they offer can be used to create eye-catching advertisements, propaganda, and to design effective interfaces for visual, textual and oral inputs/outputs. We use language to communicate information and intention. Tone, inflexion, pace, style, punctuation, sequencing, variety and gesture (body language) add layers of nuance and amplify intention. The rules of engagement and subtleties of discourse have been laid bare by social psychologists, linguisticians and social anthropologists. We can predict outcomes. If I bellow at a subordinate, compliance, resignation or resentment will be among the probable consequences. By analyzing individual speech acts and conversation pieces we may arrive at general models or metaphors of how language is used to transmit information and the effects it has on the interlocuter.

The metaphor of management as conversation has been translated into a practical tool. The Coordinator™ software developed by Flores™ is a working instantiation of this approach.[14] The office is modeled as a set of conversations; these are reduced to a five-fold schema based on Searle's[15] speech acts (promise, command, etc.). By regulating discourse Flores hopes that his software will reduce the noise in office transactions (we discuss these ideas further in chapter 3). This is a concrete example of the pragmatic instrumentation, which we use to justify the use of metaphor in information management.

Other models that can help us understand the channels and motivations which shape the ways in which individuals exchange information come from the domain of organizational behaviorists. Game theory offers a Manichean calculus of competition (*vide* the Prisoner's Dilemma[16]), which can be applied to the most trivial or serious information event. Information exchange may also be explained in terms of intuitive behavioral taxonomies, ranging from the animalistic (tit versus condor) and the theistic (Handy's gods of management[17]), through geometric models (organizational pyramids, matrix management teams, Chinese walls and quality circles) to kinship structures.

The metaphor of family allows us to speak of clans, organizational mafia, hierarchies, closed user groups, academic tribes, gatekeepers, priesthoods, insider traders, all of which are taken seriously in the practice of management.[18] The most visible tools of the information manager, computers, are spoken of in terms of generations (from first to fifth, and beyond) and families (Prime, Vax, or Cray). The pattern extends from the tangible to the intangible: disciplines have their founding fathers, who give birth to seminal papers. A bibliography is a collection of related materials, and co-citation a means of establishing the degree of bonding between document sets (in information retrieval it is common to speak of nearest neighbor). The notion of relatedness is also the basis of classification schemes and thesauri, and the parent/child relationship (inheritance) is a core concept in semantic net theory.

Warfare

Information as a weapon is a key concept in the literature of business warfare. There is a lexicon of terms like information strategy, tactical and strategic planning, corporate battle plans, information technology and competitive advantage which testifies to a belief that business, to paraphrase Talleyrand, is war fought by other means. Titles like "Business wargames," "Marketing warfare," "The information weapon" can be found in any mainstream bookshop. Information weapons may be direct and specific (logic bombs being a favored guerrilla tactic; computer viruses a kind of germ warfare), or more abstract (propaganda or misinformation). We explore this topic further in chapter 4.

Systems which are designed as weapons will have certain characteristics: they must incorporate intelligence gathering capability, rather like radar scanning, at every level; they must facilitate flexible scenario development, they must allow for rapid change of plans, they must be impenetrable (to "low flying information," hackers, spies or infiltrators). Misinformation can act as a smokescreen, or a decoy, a tactic employed frequently by governments and unscrupulous organizations. Comparisons with intelligence operations are commonplace: industrial espionage, intelligence traps, spying, concealment, encryption, scouting and reconnaissance all now find echo in the literature of information management.[19]

Property

The notion that information is property with rights of exclusion is the basis of copyright, a positive constraint which allows two basic properties of information, non-exclusivity and non-exhaustibility, to be disregarded, and allows us to treat it as a commodity like any other, where pilfering (or plagiarism) is punishable. Such commoditization creates the conditions, or context, for speculative trading in information futures, of the kind which increasingly characterizes events like the Frankfurt Book Fair.

The metaphor is more pervasive: disciplines, or special interest groups, are described in terms of domains, fields or territories of knowledge, with turf battles between players. Barriers exist between such groups (inside and outside organizations); breakthroughs, however, may occur, especially in the context of negotiation; new ground is broken by pioneers; the building blocks of knowledge are laid one on top of the other; theories are constructed, and old paradigms toppled. Just as there are estate agents or realtors, there are information brokers, who can match clients with the information they require; and just as there are property surveyors, there are information and systems auditors.

Where such metaphors and models are taken seriously, they influence systems design. Integrated office systems, for example, may overcome barriers between departments; gateway services, cross-search facilities on databases, bulletin boards and computer conferencing provide transdisciplinary and transnational access. At the level of furniture, current developments in screen and interface design are based on the premise that we will feel at home with simulated desk-top layouts, and file structures which reflect familiar non-virtual office storage (Apple Mac's folders and waste basket; Torus Tapestry's drawers and cabinets). An amusing Danish prototype for fiction retrieval uses the building (the "Bookhouse") as its central metaphor.[20]

Other properties of information make it necessary to use constructs from different fields for description and modeling. It is non-exclusive (A, B and C can share the same information and none of them will be deprived); this means that it may be difficult to exploit as a resource, where proprietary rights are an essential component of competitive edge. Constraints must be put on the dissemination of information, and these have been established historically in the use of the property metaphor, extended and confirmed as a full-blown model in copyright, patent protection laws and non-disclosure legislation.

Access to secret, proprietary or classified information must be controlled; those who handle such material must sign non-disclosure agreements, such as the Official Secrets Act, and are distinguished by special passwords: trespassers are prosecuted. The force of the metaphor has recently been reaffirmed in law: the Law Commission in the U.K. has recommended that hacking and illegal entry should be recognized as serious felonies. Prosecution has hitherto relied on oblique legislation, as theft of non-exclusive intangibles has not been admitted as a criminal category.

Traffic

Models from traffic systems can help clarify organizational information flows. Many variables must be taken into account in trying to get from A to B in the most efficient way: these may be physical, like speed, fuel consumption (miles per gallon), congestion, route, driving conditions (visibility; road holding), or control factors like police presence and the Highway Code. Some information equivalents are: delivery/ transmission rates (baud rate); processing power (millions of instructions per second), overload; reporting/enquiry practices; system transparency/opacity; degree of formalization (this allows you to get a grip on material).

There is an apparatus of regulatory forces for information: these include data protection officers; official censors; company attorneys; libel lawyers and oversight bodies like the FCC (Federal Communications Commission), SEC (Security and Exchange Commission), SIB (Securities and Investments Board) and the Press Council. The equivalents of the Highway Code are agreed standards for information presentation and exchange, such as SGML, OSI, X.25, MARC.

Optimal route planning is a major part of information systems design. Where organizational policy favors universal or open access to information, complex flow management strategies will be called for. In most cases some sort of sifting (a filter lane; toll road) will be required, with guaranteed direct access the preserve of a privileged few. A real world analogy can be found in air traffic control, where a certain set of variables (fuel reserves; traffic sector intensity; separation distances) establishes precedence for landing rights (access).

What happens if you lose your way? You take out a map; you look for signposts. Data dictionaries, graphic browsers, co-citation cluster analyses and thesauri are information maps as they display objects in relation to one another. The signposts of the information world include menus, keywords, bibliographic references and subject headings.

The transformative powers of information lead to mapping models, from set description to cartographic and navigational analogies: where are you now, where do you want to go, what do you need to know to chart a course of action? What are the current coordinates of your frame of reference and to what extent can these be changed (alternative route planning)? These coordinates will be labeled according to a particular conceptual schema, or model. The source map produced by McLaughlin and Antonoff has been applied in the corporate sector by Horton and adapted by the Information Industry Association (IIA) as a field guide [see exhibit 1.8].

EXHIBIT 1.8

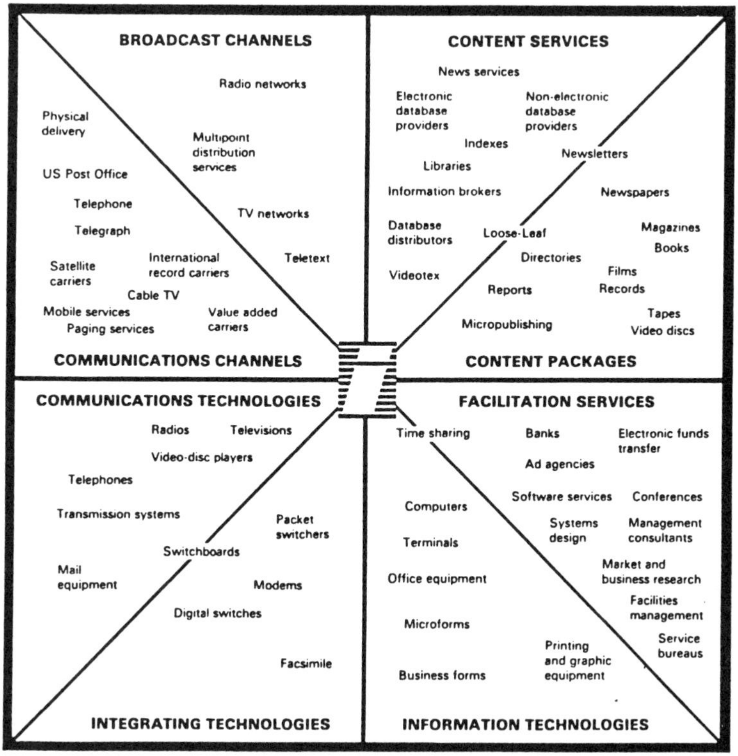

Reproduced from P. G. Zurkowski, Integrating America's infostructure. *Journal of the American Society for Information Science*, 35 (3), 1984, 170–178. Reprinted by permission of John Wiley & Sons, Inc. All rights reserved.

Manufacturing and Retailing

Manufacturing and retailing operations provide a basic model for information handling, from production to warehousing to dispatch to marketing and sales. Information is processed, in batch-mode or real-time, stored and packaged; it can be traded in the market place, has a shelf life and a scarcity value (the Knowledge Warehouse was the official title of a recent prototype electronic archiving/publishing venture in the U.K.). Documents are delivered, services must be customer driven; information can be distributed through a variety of channels from the supermarket (Dialog, the online database host, is frequently discussed in such terms) to the kiosk (like the walk-in off-campus electronic library[21]).

The fact that information is non-exhaustive (if A gives B information, A's information is not diluted) leads to a manufacturing analogy; much of the money made by commercial information entrepreneurs, and much of the value added, comes from differentiation at the processing stage (as information is not depleted, there may be no competitive edge in having access to the raw resource per se, though having priority access is a different matter), just as competing tomato growers can pull ahead by harvesting earlier, or canning and pureeing at source.

The Earth Sciences

The exploitation of natural resources is another useful source of analogy. The processes which shape the earth, above and beneath the surface, have their information equivalents. Knowledge may be described in terms of moving surfaces, like the plates of the earth, which generate activity, from local debate to paradigm shift. New landscapes may be formed where heat and pressure produce eruptions or earthquakes. Originality has its own Richter Scale, with authors, their publications and scholarly journals being ranked and assessed in terms of impacts.[22]

Archives function like sedimentary deposit, preserving the fine grain of earlier decisions and events (potential assets for the successor generation). Market research, to extend the metaphor, is based on sampling (a sample is basically a model of a population) and surveying, which allows you to prospect for new business. We write or speak in a certain vein. Information is buried in files; items are extracted, like diamonds from kimberlites, from official registers; we carry out in-depth research, and sift and filter information. Raw data, like crude oil, can be refined into different grades of product (fractionated): census data are made available at various levels of aggregation to value-added resellers. Pipelining in DP parlance ensures the smooth flow of information through the cpu; spillage is a leaked story, which may have damaging or polluting effects.

Economics and Finance

Economics deals with the allocation and utilization of scarce resources in the production and distribution of goods and services. Macro and micro models are used to describe and predict interactions and outcomes (if the interest rate rises by 2 percent, the effect on mortage repayments, house purchasing and ultimately the construction industry will be . . .). The application of econometric models, like the Cobb Douglas formula[23], is well established in the professional literature of information management; indeed, information economics is a recognized discipline in its own right, and the information economy an accepted construct with its own expanding lexicon (information worker, information occupation, information industry, information sector, information goods and services, information capital, information space, tradeable information, information broking, information observatory).

The widespread use of the resource metaphor challenges the view that information should be treated as an overhead expense (a tax-in-kind to be levied on organizational operations) and encourages profit centers/generators to treat information inputs as levers of management added value.[24]

Economic models, like those from life sciences, are used in a variety of ways. Some are directly applied. Basic input-output models can be used to describe the transformative effects of information in terms of specifically defined productivity measures at the level of the individual enterprise. At the macro level, the relative performance of nations in terms of knowledge creation can be mapped using input-output models: here the raw inputs (funds, scientific equipment, human resources) are matched against final outputs (publications, patents, discoveries).[25] This approach can be used to track a nation's market share in global science, at the general or discipline-specific level. Others are used metaphorically: for example, the exploration of more general market mechanisms as they apply to open networked information transactions or agoric systems[26]; or the notion of academic disciplines as importers and exporters of information and knowledge, with a balance of trade in ideas.[27]

Certain economic laws find their echo in information: Pareto has already been mentioned, while Gresham's Law, which states that bad money will push good out of circulation, describes the tendency for journalese, trivia, gossip, propaganda and second-rate scholarship to elbow the serious and significant into the wings.

Meaning and Malleability

We bend language to capture reality. The tools of this trade are metaphors, models, metonyms, sets and classification schema: it is they which shape our worldviews, condition our understanding of events. We source these widely, from chemistry laboratories to battle fields (exhibit 1.7 illustrates the diversity of schema in use). The resource metaphor is now used almost reflexively to describe the social and organizational significance of information, while analogies from warfare, bloodied in the corporate environment, are being adopted more widely as the ideology of competition finds fresh and often surprising adherents.

Language and worldviews are dynamic, reflecting shifts in social, economic and cultural values. Today's favored metaphor may have a limited life, as new ways of seeing and labeling our quotidian reality emerge. So too with classification systems. Just as the 1855 Bordeaux Classification of *grands crus* has been altered to take account of historic injustices, decimal schema, such as Dewey or UDC, have undergone continuous updating in the face of change. But yesterday's general classification schema now behave like inflexible corsets, squeezing and deforming knowledge in a vain attempt to represent a dynamic reality.

Classification, as we said at the beginning of this chapter, is relativistic. The miscellany of models and metaphors introduced here should not be taken too literally, or treated as being mutually exclusive. What we are offering is a kaleidoscope: it is up to you to decide which configuration has the greatest potency; which model, or models, the greatest relevance to your particular situation.

References

1. Mintzberg, H. Crafting strategy. *Harvard Business Review,* July-August 1987, 66–75; and see Mintzberg, H. *Mintzberg on management.* New York: Free Press, 1989.
2. Kuhn, T. S. *The structure of scientific revolutions.* Chicago: University of Chicago Press, 1970.
3. Cronin, B, and Davenport, E. Strategic information management. In Cronin, B. and Tudor-Silovic, N. (eds.). *The knowledge industries: levers of economic and social development in the 1990s.* London: Aslib, 1990, 45–57.
4. Merton, R. K. *The sociology of science: theoretical and empirical investigations.* Chicago: Chicago University Press, 1973.

5. Brand, S. *The media lab: inventing the future at MIT.* Harmondsworth, Eng.: Penguin, 1988.
6. Lakoff, G. *Women, fire, and dangerous things: what categories reveal about the mind.* Chicago: University of Chicago Press, 1987.
7. Burk, C. F. and Horton, F. W. *Infomap: a complete guide to discovering corporate information resources.* Englewood Cliffs, NJ: Prentice-Hall, 1988.
8. Meadows, A. J. (ed.). Introduction: *The origins of information science.* London: Taylor Graham/IIS, 1987.
9. Shannon, C. E. A mathematical theory of communication. *Bell System Technical Journal,* 27, July and October 1948, 379–423; 623-656.
10. Iselin, E. R. The impact of information diversity on information overload effects in unstructured managerial decision making. *Journal of Information Science,* 15(3), 1989, 163-173.
11. Beer, S. *Brain of the firm.* Chichester, Eng.: Wiley, 1981.
12. Dawkins, R. *The blind watchmaker.* Harlow, Eng.: Longman, 1986.
13. Nelson, T. H. *Literary machines.* San Antonio, TX: the Author, 1987.
14. Winograd, T. and Flores, F. *Understanding computers and cognition.* Norwood, NJ: Ablex, 1986.
15. Searle, J. R. *Expression and meaning: studies in the theory of speech acts.* Cambridge: Cambridge University Press, 1979.
16. Dawkins, R. *The selfish gene.* Oxford: Oxford University Press, 1989. 2nd ed. See chapter 12.
17. Handy, C. *Gods of management: how they work and why they fail.* London: Souvenir Press, 1978.
18. Becher, T. *Academic tribes and territories: intellectual enquiry and the cultures of disciplines.* Milton Keynes, Eng.: The Open University Press/The Society for Research into Higher Education, 1989.
19. Dedijer, S. and Jequier, N. (eds.). *Intelligence for economic development: an inquiry into the role of the knowledge industry.* Oxford: Berg, 1987.
20. Petjersen, A. M. The "Bookhouse": an icon based database system for fiction retrieval in public libraries. In Clausen, H. (ed.). *Information and innovation.* Proceedings of the 7th Nordic Conference for Information and Documentation, 28–30 August 1989. Aarhus: Aarhus University, 1989, 165–178.
21. Weiskel, T. C. University libraries, integrated scholarly

information systems (ISIS) and the changing character of academic research. *Library Hi Tech,* 24, 1989, 7–27.
22. Todorov, R. and Glanzel, W. Journal citation measures: a concise review. *Journal of Information Science,* 14(1), 1988, 47–56.
23. Hayes, R. M. and Erickson, T. Added value as a function of purchases of information services. *Information Society,* 1(4), 1982, 307–338.
24. Strassmann, P. A. *Information payoff: the transformation of work in the electronic age.* New York: Free Press, 1985.
25. Inhaber, H. and Alvo, M. World science as an input-output system. *Scientometrics,* 1(1), 1978, 43–64.
26. Miller, M. S. and Drexler, K. E. Markets and computation: agoric open systems. In Huberman, B. A. (ed.). *The ecology of computation.* New York: Elsevier, 1988, 51–76.
27. Cronin, B. and Davenport, L. Profiling the professors. *Journal of Information Science,* 15(1), 1989, 13–20.

2
MOBILIZING ASSETS

Information Assets

Chapter one introduced a number of focal metaphors and models: here we explore the significance of the asset metaphor and how it might be operationalized. An asset is something owned by an individual or organization which confers, or might be expected to confer, economic benefit to its owner, and whose value can be expressed in monetary terms. Assets can be of various kinds: current or fixed; tangible or intangible. Exhibit 2.1 is a model which classifies the assets of an organization in conventional fashion. The concept can be extended, however, to include social benefits, such as are conferred by public assets.

If information is an asset, it may be viewed from a number of perspectives: as a public, merit or private good. Public goods are those which generate community benefits, like an AIDS awareness program, and are subsidized. Merit goods combine direct benefits to those who pay (partial subsidy) with wider social benefits: "not only was the U.S. the first nation to attempt to approve scientifically the productivity of farms through systematic research, but it was also the first nation to recognize the benefits to society of having that information as widely distributed as possible . . . easy access to low cost information made it possible for advances on the farm to lead to the industrial age and subsequent prosperity."[1] Private goods, by way of contrast, benefit only those individuals who are willing and able to pay [see exhibit 2.2].

EXHIBIT 2.1

Assets

	TANGIBLE	INTANGIBLE
CURRENT	Cash Debtors Stock	Personnel
FIXED	Property Plant	Goodwill

The perspective taken will obviously influence a manager's interpretation of what constitutes an information asset.

Our basic matrix is labeled in classic accounting terms. Tangible current assets would include cash-in-hand, outstanding debts and existing stock, and a company's net current assets would be the sum of these minus outstanding liabilities. Quick current assets are cash and items which are readily convertible into cash. Intangible current assets include the organization's human resources. In the case of a management consulting firm these will constitute the organization's major assets. These assets can leak unless efforts are made to keep them sweet with staff development, job enrichment and career planning programs. The wounds inflicted may be severe: a recent insider has told how Salomon Brothers "[b]y

EXHIBIT 2.2

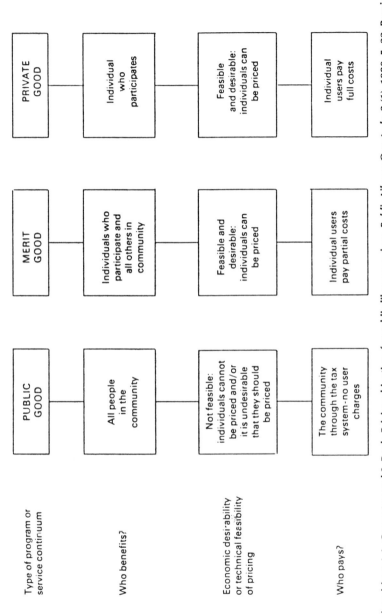

Type of program or service continuum	PUBLIC GOOD	MERIT GOOD	PRIVATE GOOD
Who benefits?	All people in the community	Individuals who participate and all others in community	Individual who participates
Economic desirability or technical feasibility of pricing	Not feasible: individuals cannot be priced and/or it is undesirable that they should be priced	Feasible and desirable: individuals can be priced	Feasible and desirable: individuals can be priced
Who pays?	The community through the tax system—no user charges	Individual users pay partial costs	Individual users pay full costs

Reproduced from J. L. Crompton and S. Bonk, Pricing objectives for public library services. *Public Library Quarterly*, 2 (1), 1980, 5–22. Reprinted by permission of The Haworth Press, Inc., 10 Alice Street, Binghamton, NY 13904.

allowing dozens of able mortgage traders to fertilize the mortgage departments of other firms . . . let slip through its fingers the rarest and most valuable asset a Wall Street firm can possess: a monopoly."[2] This principle applies more widely: historically, professional football teams have written off transfer fees, but the trend now is to enter this kind of expenditure as an intangible asset on the balance sheet.

An enterprise's fixed tangible assets typically include land, property, plant and vehicles, some of which may depreciate. Our fourth category is fixed intangible. In the U.S., for example, companies are required to write off or amortize goodwill. Goodwill, also referred to as going concern value, is treated separately from physical assets under current accounting practice and viewed as a fixed intangible. However, goodwill, unlike machinery, is an asset which could retain its value indefinitely, if properly managed.

The Three Conditions

Our three conditions for information management are that it can be modeled, modeled in a context, and for a purpose. What expectations and insights are stimulated by the asset metaphor? We look at four contexts: business, government, the university campus and libraries, which involve both public and private assets. The objective of asset management in each of these cases is to realize the latent value of information resources.

Just how might this be achieved? The simple act of classifying and labeling information entities and resources in terms of attributes appropriate to the four quadrants may reveal potential. Or, resources may migrate from one quadrant to another, if made tangible (expertise embodied in software, for example). Our 2 × 2 matrix can also be used as an outline investment guide where the depreciation associated with a hard investment, like network technology, is offset by intangible benefits in terms of connectivity.

Opacity and Transparency

Information assets are embodied in services, systems and human expertise. Our ability to exploit these will depend on whether they are opaque or transparent. Opacity may be unintentional: features like poor design, excessive bureaucracy, technical jargon, complex pricing mechanisms and confusing access procedures may detract from the value of what is on offer. But opacity may also be contrived: game theory relies on strategies and counter strategies, and many political systems depend on such concealment. And priesthoods (literal and figurative) use ritual, rites of passage and private language (the Tridentine Mass; the convoluted syntax of the legal profession) to preserve status and monopolistic practices. Mystique, in professional life, is often little more then cleverly cultivated opacity. This is as true of information management as any other professional domain.

The acceptable levels of opacity and transparency in any system will be context-dependent. In some cases, opaque systems disenfranchise potential beneficiaries and create conditions which nurture questionable or corrupt practices, while perfectly transparent systems may result in overload. As a general rule, lack of transparency results in sub-optimal use of information assets, whether in the cause of improved profitability or economic development. However, by identifying the generic attributes of transparent and opaque systems, you will be better positioned to exploit information assets. Exhibits 2.3 and 2.4 list some of the core attributes. We characterize transparent systems in terms of standardization (modes of access, enquiry, structuring and reporting which conform to agreed norms), openness (freely available), structural clarity (ease of navigation, whether in a database or a technical information center) and a minimum of rules.

Opaque systems favor local idioms (multiple command languages; incompatible classification schemes; different operating systems), are not blessed with a paucity of rules,

EXHIBIT 2.3
Transparent Systems

Openness	Primary characteristic
Standards Equal access Disclosure	Secondary characteristics
Clear Structure Few rules Few media transformations	Conditions
Accountability Effective interaction High skills transfer Widespread adoption	Effects

EXHIBIT 2.4
Opaque Systems

Closure	Primary characteristic
Local idioms Elitism Suppression	Secondary characteristics
Lack of structural clarity Excessive regulation **Many media transformations**	Conditions
Fudging Muddling through Low skills transfer Limited adoption	Effects

and exclude certain groups (non-initiates; laymen; the economically disadvantaged). By extension, opaque systems (whether we are talking about a data processing department or a scholarly research library) are elitist: the level of use remains artificially, or willfully, depressed (exclusivity creates marketing edge).

Transparent systems encourage efficiency by minimizing the number of media transformations required in any routine transaction, be it processing a new membership request, clearing a bank check or replenishing inventory. They foster widespread use (Minitel in France or CompuServe in the U.S.) and promote skills transfer throughout the adopter population. Egalitarianism is a key feature: transparent systems are designed for popular rather than restricted use, whether in corporate headquarters or the local social welfare office.

Levels of Transparency

Our transparency/opacity indicators can be used at different levels. They may guide a primary analysis of a whole economy. De Soto has recently described the role of the black economy in Peru where "informal" activities account for 60 percent of employment and 40 percent of the domestic product.[3] Informal activities emerge from a desire to beat the system, where bureaucracy is top-heavy and impenetrable. Bureaucracy, Weber points out[4], thrives on secrecy, and this *per se* is a source of opacity, which may be manifest as lack of public accountability. In the early 1980s the scale of investment in West Germany's Specialized Information and Documentation Program was criticized by the General Audit Office. More recently, questions have been raised about the capital and recurrent costs of supporting the CEC's ECHO (European Commission Host Organization) databases.

At a more local level (in, say, a government department like the IRS in the U.S. or the DHSS in the U.K.) traditional methods of documentation, intended originally as agents of transparency, now inhibit exploitation of an increasingly complex and vastly expanded document base. In such cases, manuals and procedural guidelines will be produced, but they themselves may ossify into agents of opacity. Library cataloging illustrates the point. If the process conforms to the highest level of detail recommended in the standard manual, the Anglo-American Cataloging Rules (AACR), specialist staff will be required. And if the product (catalog entry) reflects such detail, it will not be transparent to the majority of users. Professionalism also satisfies most of our criteria of opacity: it produces an elite, defined in terms of mastery of complex rules, who sustain their position by controlling access *(numerus clausus)* and turbidity.

Dealing with Opacity

How do you cope with an opaque system? You can try to make it transparent. Simplifying and filtering are mechanisms: short catalog entries in the library context; expert systems of the types used in government departments.[5] In medicine, expert systems can bypass first instance professional consultation by accepting input from the layman and proffering appropriate advice. Intelligent front-ends to databases bypass information intermediaries in the same way.

Where an opaque system fails to respond to reasonable demands, its users may seek alternative sources or outlets, another form of bypass. Informal economies and alternative cultures are not confined to nation states; they may be found in systems at any level. Patients may ask a friend who is a nurse for health advice which they can understand; students will ask their peers what to read; researchers plug into invisible colleges.

The indicators in exhibits 2.3 and 2.4 can be used to compare your existing system or service with others in the marketplace in terms of transparency and opacity, at the surface or deep level. This should also prompt a series of "what if?" questions, designed to tease out alternative courses of action for delivering greater value from the existing asset base to target constituencies.

Business Information

Every enterprise is driven by information: information on environmental trends and issues, products, markets, standards, procedures, regulations and customers. In addition it exploits data on its own internal performance and functioning (order fulfillment, capacity utilization, market share, cash flow, absenteeism levels). Which of these data sets, or which systems and services, can be fitted to the asset matrix? How can a company convert subsistence information into high-yield information which impacts on the bottom line?

We have highlighted some generic business information assets in exhibit 2.5. Consider the case of a manager who wishes to realize the full asset value of customer information files. If these are located in the tangible assets quadrant they can be used for market segmentation and advertising, for monitoring and profiling consumer spending and for test marketing new services and products. Such data are obviously a rich source of insight, and they also save money, used internally in lieu of commissioned market studies, or sold to interested third parties, such as list-building agencies in the direct mail advertising industry.

A company's fixed tangible information assets include the telecommunications infrastructure (leased lines, value-added services, switching gear, satellite links) and the installed hardware and systems base: a company with spare computer processing or line capacity can move into facilities management or set up its own managed data network to compete with established players in the lucrative telecommunications marketplace. Such an approach may allow a company to plough back revenues which are offset against capital costs.

EXHIBIT 2.5

Business Information Assets

	TANGIBLE	INTANGIBLE
CURRENT	Competitor files Customer databases	Corporate memory EDI- links Copyright
FIXED	Telecoms backbone Information systems	Trademarks

Encapsulated Know-how

The collective know-how of a business (its corporate memory) should be counted as a current intangible. The experience and heuristics of personnel, company lore and precedent have latent value which under certain conditions can be assigned a monetary equivalent, whether in terms of internal benefits (time and labor savings through not hiring external trainers/consultants) or external benefits where the company becomes a supplier of expertise to the outside world. However, these assets can depreciate in several ways; disaffection, obsolescence, senescence. To prevent atrophy and optimize performance, a company must nurture its human resources.

The encapsulation of expertise in knowledge-based systems, registers, codes of conduct or procedural manuals can reduce opacity. They make explicit or transparent what was implicit, and accelerate the transfer of talent through an organization. Patents, copyrights and registered designs also reduce opacity by recording or trapping proprietary know-how and releasing it to a wider constituency beyond the bounds of the company. We place them, however, in the current intangible quadrant. They are current because the protection they offer is finite, and they are intangible because usage and thus monetary returns are unpredictable. The other entry in this quadrant, electronic data interchange (EDI), entails the linking of nodes in a buyer-supplier network for information exchange. We have labeled it intangible because it represents an abstraction, connectivity, rather than the nuts and bolts of the system.

Trademarks, like hallmarks, are fixed intangible assets. A name which elicits customer loyalty can, as recent experience shows, boost goodwill in accounting terms at a time of take-over. Kraft with its battery of long-established house-hold brands, boosted its new parent's (Philip Morris) goodwill asset sheet by £11 billion. And the trademark Jaguar, with its aura of craftsmanship, inspired engineering and high quality, accounted for most of the £1.6 billion price paid by Ford. Unlike other protection mechanisms, such as patents, trade-marks and brand names can be sustained indefinitely and retain their asset value.

Marketing Information

Our matrix can be applied to the information assets of a large manufacturing company, either at the level of the entire organization, or at the level of the strategic business unit (SBU) or functional activity. Marketing and Sales, for example, might wish to minimize the cost per order dollar (cpod): the critical success factor in this division is securing the maximum number of orders at the lowest possible cost. What are the information assets which must be deployed to achieve this objective?

Commercial intelligence is a primary asset. At the macro level, markets must be monitored and analyzed in terms of competitor activity and intention, externalities like exchange rates or fiscal policy, and opportunities to launch new products or expand the customer base. Much of this information is sourced from publicly available services (business information databases, trend indicators, market digests, social attitude surveys, trade newsletters). However, because it is widely available, it can only offer limited competitive advantage (other companies can access it too), but customized and contoured for the company's field salesforce directors and business sector managers it may function as an asset.

Customization is the key, and *table d'hôte* provision is giving way to *à la carte* profiles of the strengths and weaknesses of established and emergent competitors within industry. Given the wealth of experience and embedded industry know-how scattered throughout the organization, public sources provide relatively little that is new: they confirm rather than illuminate. It is the quality of the processing or "cooking" which adds value to the asset.

Tracking Transformations

Exhibit 2.6 is a simple kite figure which can be used to track the process of adding value. The present application is impressionistic, though quantifiable coordinates could be used to turn it into a more exact instrument of measurement. The two-dimensional space shows a company's (or unit's) information orientation; the horizontal axis defines the degree of value added (from raw to well cooked) and the vertical, the relative emphasis on strategic versus support information. In this illustration, we suggest a development strategy for a company which was under-exploiting its assets and was content to deliver raw information of the support kind.

In general terms, this means giving greater attention to

EXHIBIT 2.6
Use of Information Assets

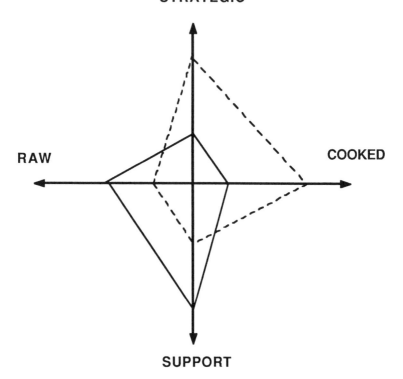

STRATEGIC

RAW   COOKED

SUPPORT

Legend:

Current   _____

Suggested _ _ _ _ _ _ _ _ _

value-adding activities (issue management, digesting and analysis, customization, design of simplified access protocols) and to identifying inputs and activities which would have a strategic impact on business development. Such a change in emphasis might require a shift from broadband provision (standard outputs for one and all) to narrowcasting (targeting key clients and work groups with bespoke services), perhaps in the shape of a deal tracking system covering critical incidents in the negotiation which precedes an order (installation of a pilot system, knockout of a rival bidder, emergence of a strong competitor). If such information is structured and standardized it can transform routinely harvested insight and experience into an asset.

Information requirements within companies vary across client sectors: for instance, the information sets which define accounts in aerospace differ from those in pharmaceutics. Sector-specific account plans are used to generate structured profiles of key potential customers, based on standard company information (main lines of business, subsidiaries, turnover), industry norms (for expenditure on information systems) and key financial indicators (current assets, stock, employee count, return on sales). Asset value can be enhanced when data from commercially available sources are complemented by information on procurement policies and practices (sign-off procedures, authorized signatories, financial limits) in addition to a range of softer information on culture, ethos, business style and stance. Such profiles would also include an assessment of industry-specific market thrusts, opportunities and threats.

Body Talk

In exhibit 2.7 we group the various categories of company-related information under three headings: public presence (standard indicators of current performance and market position); public posture (formal signals and statements of intent), and body language (how an organization actually

EXHIBIT 2.7

PUBLIC PRESENCE	PUBLIC POSTURE	BODY LANGUAGE
Sales turnover	Annual reports	Corporate culture
Pre tax earnings	Press coverage	Budget cycle
Shareholder dividends	Press releases	Management style
Current assets	Advertising	Organizational style
Debtors	Public relations	Business stance
Return on net assets	Exhibitions	Procurement style
Return on sales	Philanthropy	
Stock turnover	Hi/low tech image	
Sales per employee	Hospitality	
P/e ratio	Unionization	
ROI	Sponsorship	
Gearing		

behaves). This three-part checklist can be used in any context, wherever there is a need to profile the players in a field. Public presence and public posture information are recognized as sources of business intelligence; body language, however, is often neglected.

In the context of sales and marketing, body language will be defined in terms of observation and face-to-face dealings with a range of contacts in client companies. Such information can be trapped and tapped with a sales force automation program.[6] Providing direct access to a range of external and company databases for information on customers, current stock levels, order status reports, delivery lead times might be the initial motivation [see exhibit 2.8]. Lap-tops are more than access tools, however: they can function as instruments for the capture of soft information (what we earlier described as body language) which can then be disseminated and shared more widely.

Field Information

Field information is rarely exploited in a systematic or comprehensive way. Input may be seen as an added burden,

EXHIBIT 2.8

Databases	Catalogues	Ordering	E-mail	Doc.creation	Diary	Apps.s/ware
Quotas	Phone nos.	Configs.	Files	Letters	Schedules	Spreadsheets
Customer info.	Price lists	Order status	Memos	OHTs	Seminars	Personal libr.
Industry norms	Products	Deliveries	SWOTs	Expenses	Visits	Graphics
Competitor data		Procurement				
Ref.site data						
Hand-over data						
PIPs						
Kompass						
Corporate culture						
Recent IT spend						
Personal files						

though it is clear that the exchange of significant and timely detail can be of immediate practical advantage where it removes the Chinese walls which inhibit lateral information flows between different accounts or regions. Such a network allows individuals to leverage off one another's experience. The end-result is an aggregate of shared know-how/know-who, which can be quarried at other levels in an organization: a marketing department or a training unit.

In this illustration, the company is simply harnessing customer-related information which is informally or osmotically acquired by its personnel in the course of their working lives and combining it with other data culled from published and electronic sources. It is the process of structuring and integrating this collective know-how that converts the raw into the cooked, which can be shared and digested by a wide range of users.

Campus Information

"Top universities . . . are vying for top quality students and professors in much the same way that top corporations are battling for the best MBA graduates. The university, however, does not have partnerships, six-figure salaries, or profit bonuses at its disposal. What it does have are computers."[7] This is the environment we have in mind in our discussion of campus information assets: a highly competitive and highly computerized arena.

Exhibit 2.9 illustrates some campus information assets. In many respects, a university is like a factory: it is in the knowledge engineering and fabrication business. The raw inputs are experimental and survey data, received wisdom, information: the outputs are new models, theorems, paradigms, techniques, processes, discoveries, which can be embodied in a variety of forms, ranging from journal articles, through patents to commercial software packages.

EXHIBIT 2.9

Campus Information Assets

	TANGIBLE	INTANGIBLE
CURRENT	Specialist knowledge bases Research publications Courseware	Invisible colleges Consultancy skills
FIXED	Laboratories Libraries Computer centre Networks	Hallmark

A university's current tangible information assets consist of its proprietary knowledge stock; the specialist databases created or hosted by the institution; the publications produced by its community of scholars and researchers; monographs and serials printed by the university press; bibliographic files and data sets accumulated by research teams; packaged educational and training materials, and courseware. Its tangible fixed information assets include the university library and its satellites, the computer center and the sunk infrastructural investment in local and wide area networks. Laboratories may be included in this class as they constitute the locus of measurement, data capture and analysis.[8]

The Invisible College

Invisible colleges and information networks are information assets; current and intangible. These can be tapped to provide early warning of new intellectual developments or windows of commercial opportunity (a list of alumni transformed into a structured database becomes a powerful marketing tool for fund-raising purposes). The expertise of scholars is also an asset: universities are well positioned to capitalize on the marketable know-how of the human resource through consultancy and industry-academe links.

What's in a name? A seal of quality: Oxford, Princeton, Cambridge and Harvard are hallmarks and provide as much comparative advantage as the assay mark of a silversmith. Information goods and services thus branded have an edge. Hallmark is an intangible fixed asset, the university equivalent of corporate goodwill.

Our four campus information assets can be relocated onto the mobilization matrix shown in exhibit 2.10, the purpose of which is to relate three classes of impact (improved efficiency, enhanced effectiveness, transformation) to asset type and location within the overall system (at the level of infrastructure, operations or the marketplace).

Competing on Campus

Suppose a university in a competitive educational environment chooses to compete on price by cutting costs (which in turn may be reflected in lower admission and tuition fees). Its information systems investment strategy will concentrate on the bottom left-hand corner of the matrix at the intersection of efficiency and infrastructure. A university may use its fixed assets (information systems) to improve cost efficiency in processing of student applications, in handling student registration data and in coordinating its examination and

EXHIBIT 2.10
Asset Mobilization Matrix

INFRASTRUCTURE OPERATIONS MARKETS

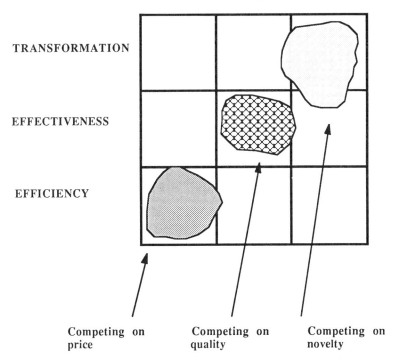

TRANSFORMATION

EFFECTIVENESS

EFFICIENCY

Competing on price   Competing on quality   Competing on novelty

Based on an idea from G. Peters, quoted in D. Finkelstein, Cashing in on WANS. *Network,* December 1987, 6–10.

grading systems. In this scenario, the quality of its core operations (teaching and research) is not materially affected, but its back-of-house systems work more smoothly and salary costs are pared back.

An alternative scenario has the objective of differentiation (competing on novelty), not lower unit costs. In this case assets are deployed in the upper right-hand corner of the matrix at the point where transformation and markets intersect. A university might exploit its information assets (courseware) by taking value-added products into new markets. Commercial satellite communication systems and video conferencing would allow it to capture remote markets ahead of its rivals. The strategic deployment of assets in this way totally transforms the educational delivery process and has a major impact on the marketplace.

A third scenario (competing on quality) focuses on the center quadrant where effectiveness and operations overlap. A university would here use its fixed assets to increase the effectiveness of one or more of its core operations, for example, research. These might include advanced workstations, a supercomputer link or a fiber optic network, encouraging computer-supported collaborative work across disciplinary and institutional boundaries.

The scramble for external research funding may entail profiling of sponsors (grant-awarding bodies, research councils, charitable foundations or industrial partners) on the lines suggested in our public presence/public posture/body language matrix [exhibit 2.7] and tracking the growing number of RFPs (requests for proposals) from national and international agencies. Much of the relevant information is already circulating within the system, but is highly dispersed and often internalized. Like salesforce know-how it will remain underexploited until it is systematized.

Post-Professionalism

Historically, libraries have been the acknowledged centers of information activities on campus. Where this mindset prevails it will be difficult to liberalize information assets, as information will be narrowly identified with one constituency, colored by a particular professional outlook. Indeed, it might be argued that professionalism has inhibited the exploitation of information assets on campus.[9] But there are signs of change. Bridges are being built between information islands in the academic archipelago, and terms like convergence, integration, holistic planning and information utility have entered the campus vernacular. Connectivity is the key to activating the partitioned and neglected information assets dispersed throughout the university system.

Government Data

Government is the major gatherer and disseminator of information. We explore its asset potential in this chapter and examine the economics of the government data market more fully in chapter 5. Under current tangible in exhibit 2.11 we include publications emanating from official agencies such as

EXHIBIT 2.11

Government Data Assets

	TANGIBLE	INTANGIBLE
CURRENT	Publications Time series data	Scale and scope
FIXED	Government Data Network (GDN)	Crown copyright

the Government Printing Office (GPO) or Her Majesty's Stationery Office (HMSO) and the vast array of time series data (trade, demographic, labor) and census information which is routinely harvested, warehoused and retailed. A major intangible asset for government is the scale and scope of the information activities it carries out in support of its regulatory, policy, auditing and social reporting functions. Its hand is everywhere, giving it incomparable access to a multiplicity of information sources.

Its principal fixed intangible (in the U.K. at least) is crown copyright, the legal framework within which its information asset base is rooted. This enabling mechanism creates enormous scope for developing and exploiting information, whether produced inside government, gathered from taxpayers, compiled by regulatory bodies, volunteered by industry or submitted by government-funded researchers. A fixed tangible asset in the U.K. is the Government Data Network (GDN): fixed in terms of cabling and hardware; tangible because, theoretically, its value could be realized in a commercial sale.

Exhibit 2.11 provides some examples of government data assets: publications, and time series datasets. The list can be extended to include general Household Survey data (in the U.K.), the General Election Surveys, specialist census data like the sets which emanate from the Ministry of Agriculture, Fisheries and Food (MAFF).

Commercial Exploitation

Many of these are exploited commercially, though only a few are offered on direct access to the public. In an age of networked bureaucracy the risks are too high. The time series data of the Central Statistical Office (CSO), for example, are offered on a three-tier basis. They may be sent for directly, distributed in a comparatively raw state on tape or microfiche;

they may be accessed through the national data archive which is sponsored by the ESRC (Economic and Social Research Council) online or in tape form. In this case they may have have value added in the form of customized preparation to fit a particular set of access codes, or machine-specific processing software. Alternatively, they may be accessed in gourmet form, as it were, through one of the major commercial online vendors: CSO data are major files offered by Jordans and ICC, bearing the full panoply of facilities (downloading, cross-file searching, integration into other software) which such hosts provide.

The marketing of census data in the U.K. is conducted on a similar three-tier basis. Data may be obtained directly from the OPCS (Office of Public Censuses and Surveys); they may be accessed through the Essex Data Archive (on a similar basis to CSO's offerings), or they may be exploited through one of the commercial agencies which support market research, like CACI Inc., who have derived detailed house-hold classifications (the Acorn system) from their analysis of census material.

As we have seen, much of the data is held at source (within government departments) in raw form, or in a state of nature. Its asset value will depend on several factors. The first is government monopoly and the fact that the information is unobtainable elsewhere. The second has to do with the range and volume of materials; even in a raw state, such holdings offer economies of scope. Yet, the desirability of government monopoly is being questioned in the U.K. and the market for official statistics is being liberalized.

Value-Added Reselling

The asset value of raw data is limited, but can be enhanced by processing. If source departments are unable or unwilling to do this themselves, the case in most U.K. government agencies, they must contract out to a third party, either subsidized or operating on a fully commercial basis (the model guidelines provided by the Department of Trade and Industry [DTI] are discussed further in chapter 5). The mechanisms for this include franchises and royalty payments, the charges for which will vary: a government committed to the free market may encourage its agencies to seek maximum returns to cover the costs of collection and overhead, and future investment. At present in the U.K., departments are advised to cover the costs of collection, but not overheads, though this is seen by some as the start of a process which will attenuate the role of government in the collection of statistics to choreography or coordination of a group of independent commercial agencies.

Ideology apart, there may be good reasons for this approach. Security is one. Access to the Government Data Network, even to non-sensitive, non-controversial files, is considered a potential security risk in the U.K. By purchasing information from a private vendor, government can satisfy its requirements and obviate the need to provide public access, since other interested parties are themselves free to deal with the same vendor. Headcount is another. Why sustain at the public expense an operation which can be handled privately?

The downside is the fate of data sets which are unattractive in market terms and unlikely to interest commercial developers. The British General Election Survey had difficulty in finding commercial support when the government withheld ESRC (Economic and Social Research Council) funding in 1983. If this could happen to "the most widely used data set in Britain," what will be the fate of more *recherché* files?[10]

What is the asset potential of document as opposed to data sets (technical reports, regulatory material, statutory instruments, parliamentary or congressional information, for example)? Unless such material is held in electronic form, it remains an under-exploited asset, as the cake cannot be sliced in as many ways as digitized material.

Public and Private Goods

Up to this point we have assumed that government information can be treated as a private good. This is the tenor of current government thinking in the U.K., supported by a raft of policy documents and initiatives. In the U.S., government information is seen primarily as a public good: a recent (June 1989) statement from the Office of Management and Budget (OMB) sustains federal commitment to a "fundamental philosophy . . . that government information is a public asset" and that "it is the obligation of the government to make such information readily available to the public on equal terms to all citizens."[11] This reaffirms the obligations of government which are set out in the First Amendment and in the Freedom of Information legislation.

A public asset is not defined exclusively in terms of monetary equivalence. In the U.S. there is a mission to inform citizenry and a willingness to acknowledge the existence of positive externalities: an example quoted earlier is the provision of AIDS information through the federal depository library network on the grounds that the wider the dissemination of the information, the greater people's awareness of the risks, and the fewer the cases of the disease.

In exhibit 2.12 we look at some of the options for access to U.S. Bureau of the Census data. Keen as the commitment is to ensure public access on equal terms, there is a countervailing imperative to allow free enterprise to exploit census information. Purveyance as a result takes various forms. There are subsidized public agencies (National Technical Information Service [NTIS] and Inter University Consortium for Political and Social Research [ICPSR]) and there are fully commercial vendors like Dialog, the established online host, and CACI, which adds value to raw census data for market research and analysis in the U.S. and the U.K.

We have left the upper lefthand quadrant blank in our matrix: in the U.S. it is unlikely that a major government data

EXHIBIT 2.12

Access to U.S. Census Data

	PRIVATE CONTRACTOR	PUBLIC AGENCY
PRODUCER		US Bureau of the Census
PROVIDER	DIALOG CACI	NTIS ICPSR

set such as the census would be contracted out for private collection; in the U.K., however, such a scenario is not implausible if current policy trends are carried to their logical conclusions.

Libraries

We illustrate the relevance of the asset model to libraries with a large multi-type metropolitan system. This may be a fully subsidized service, or one required to generate revenues to cover a proportion of its costs. Where cost recovery is an objective, tangible fixed assets include not only the installed hardware base, but library premises (whether freehold or leased), off-site stores and fleets of mobiles [see exhibit 2.13]. Current assets include core stock and special collections, unless exploitation or disposal in either case is constrained by the terms of a bequest or endowment. The knowledgeability and professional skills of library personnel are current intangibles. They have a direct influence on levels of use and customer satisfaction. Expertise in such areas as indexing, information retrieval, knowledge engineering, online searching, historical bibliography, conservation, records management, information analysis and systems design can be marketed in the form of consultancy packages, or used as a platform to launch joint public/private sector initiatives in areas where, for example, the library has unique or proprietary materials, but lacks production,

EXHIBIT 2.13
Library Assets

	TANGIBLE	INTANGIBLE
CURRENT	Book stock Special collections	Quality of service Staff know-how
FIXED	Library premises Mobiles	Legal deposit

packaging, distribution, marketing or merchandizing capability. The convention of legal deposit is also an important information asset, whether applied to indigenously published monographs, certain classes of federal government reports, or the output of international/inter-governmental agencies (UNESCO, CEC). Legal deposit implies a collection of certain scope and size: this in turn implies quality and it may be seen as the equivalent of hallmark or trademark in the fixed intangible quadrant. Since it is selectively and sparingly conferred, it affords an advantage in terms of collection development opportunities.

A Management Matrix

We have identified a portfolio of generic information assets, both tangible and intangible, in the business, government, campus and library contexts. How can these assets be exploited to best effect? What kind of tools has the information manager at his disposal to assess the options?

Take the library, for example. What does a librarian do? Traditionally the emphasis has been on the management of *functions,* from information identification and acquisition through processing and retrieval to communication. The asset model will shift the librarian's perspective. The six key assets managed by a library director are stock, property, professional skills, goodwill, the installed information technology/information systems base, and heritage items [see exhibit 2.14].

Stock is of two kinds: current stock refers to circulating and up-to-date reference material: as in a supermarket, it includes fast turnover goods (bestsellers), premium price products (online searches) and slow-moving items (minority appeal texts); materials with a short shelf life or use-by-date (directories), warehoused goods (off-site reserve collections). Its quotidian character distinguishes it from heritage items. The nature and scope of a library's everyday stock shape

EXHIBIT 2.14

Two Perspectives

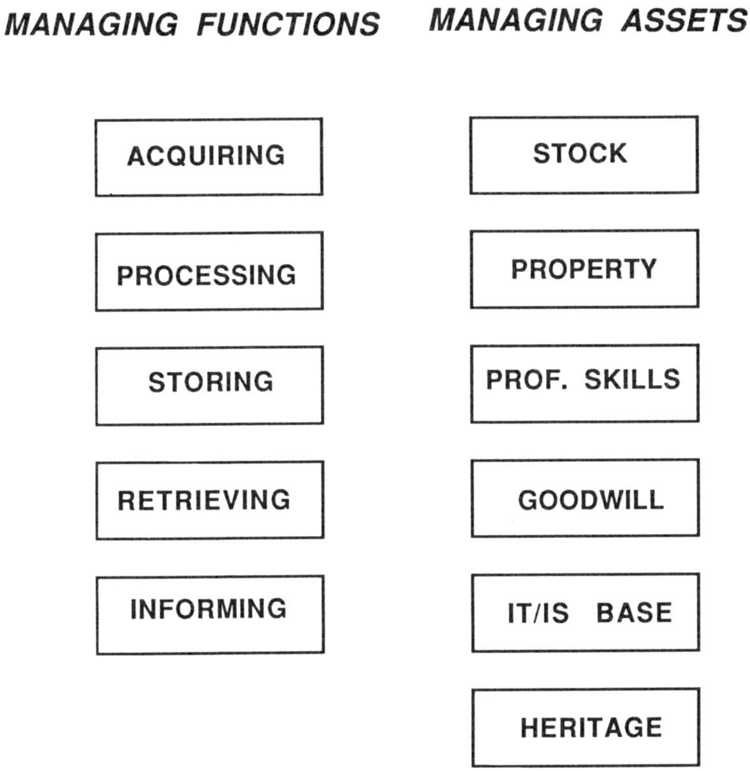

MANAGING FUNCTIONS   *MANAGING ASSETS*

ACQUIRING	STOCK
PROCESSING	PROPERTY
STORING	PROF. SKILLS
RETRIEVING	GOODWILL
INFORMING	IT/IS BASE
	HERITAGE

public reaction; shelving, classification and presentation affect propensity to use; management information derived from automated circulation control systems allows stock to be selected and deployed more effectively. Such material is a working current asset.

The asset value of heritage stock or patrimony is different. This category includes materials which are unique, difficult to replicate, or not widely accessible to the public at large. Examples range from collections of turn-of-the-century photographs, diaries and letters of famous men and women, rare monographs, special collections (political pamphlets, emblems), through newspaper collections to in-house databases on local institutions, events, personalities and facilities, and hyper/multimedia systems which integrate theme materials (theatre—history, bibliography, biography, interviews, footage, memorabilia). It is the rarity or scarcity factor, and the leverage thus implied, which allows heritage products and services to be viewed as information assets.

Asset Management Strategies

The matrix in exhibit 2.15 relates the six generic assets above to a number of broad managerial options. These range from outright disposal (selling off the family silver, in effect, to raise cash for new services or projects, to maintain existing levels of provision or to generate the funds needed to preserve core collections) to contracting out specific operating functions (as required of U.S. federal government information agencies or as advocated by the Minister of Arts & Libraries in the U.K. for public libraries). The options are not mutually exclusive; as a result of reappraising a special collection or service in terms of its current asset value, the library may seek to enter into a franchise agreement with a commercial vendor/distributor as a means of reaching a new or expanded market.

We placed property under the fixed current quandrant in exhibit 2.1. If the library (strictly speaking, the parent local authority or community) owns its sites, it has the option of selling off the property to the highest bidder, or, alternatively, entering into a lease-back arrangement which not only provides a cash injection, but guarantees tenancy for an agreed period. The management of property portfolios is a live issue for a growing number of public sector bodies in the U.K., library authorities included.[12]

Exhibit 2.16 lists a number of management strategies and the associated benefits. In the case of the disposal option

EXHIBIT 2.15

ASSET MANAGEMENT MATRIX					
OPTION	STOCK PROPERTY	PROF. SKILLS	GOODWILL	IS/IT	HERITAGE BASE
DISPOSAL					
LEASING					
FRANCHISE					
CONTRACT OUT					
REVALUE					
EXPLOIT					

(outright sale or lease-back) the library secures working or development capital which allows it to refurbish existing premises or to focus on the expansion of priority services and programs. As a less radical option, space could be franchised to a social welfare agency (citizens advice/rights bureau, consumer or legal information center, adult literacy project) or to a private company (information broker, financial analyst, bookseller, travel agent). This would improve revenues and offer patrons a richer mix of services (with the attendant synergies) delivered from a single site (the *galleria* concept in high street retailing). Sponsorship is another option, one which minimizes the risk of asset dilution through loss of

EXHIBIT 2.16

PROPERTY ASSETS	
STRATEGY	*BENEFITS*
DISPOSAL	Working capital Relocation
LEASE-BACK	Development capital
FRANCHISE	Revenue stream Improved product mix
SPONSORSHIP	Refurbishment Patron appeal

ownership or direct control. The drawback, however, is the short-term commitment favored by most sponsoring bodies.

In our role as consultants, we have seen how effective this 6×6 matrix can be in a number of practical workshop sessions with a database host, national library, university library system, regional bibliographic network, oil industry information center and research council to highlight a diversity of hidden information assets, ranging from large historic databases of geological data with overseas market potential to a unique and underexploited collection of materials on the contemporary literary life of a developing nation.

The importance of the asset metaphor lies not just in the fact that it can point up soft, undervalued or low-yield information assets: it also focuses managerial attention on the need to "ascertain the optimum choice of assets and asset configuration."[13] In many organizations, the total life-cycle costs of information goods and services are not properly understood. Unless all significant net expenditures arising during the ownership of an information asset (from database to technical journal) are explicitly acknowledged and incorporated into trade-off analyses, resources will continue to be allocated under false pretenses.

References

1. Kent, C. A. The privatizing of government information: economic considerations. *Government Publications Review,* 16(2), 1989, 113–132.
2. Lewis, M. *Liar's poker: two cities, true greed.* London: Hodder & Stoughton, 1989.
3. Main, J. How to make rich countries poor. *Fortune,* January 16, 1989, 73–75.
4. Weber, M. *The theory of social and economic organization.* New York: Free Press, 1947.
5. See for example: Duffin, P. H. (ed.). *Knowledge based systems: applications in administrative government.* Chichester, Eng.: Ellis Horwood, 1988.
6. Moriarty, R. T. and Swartz, G. S. Automation to boost sales and marketing. *Harvard Business Review,* January–February 1989, 100–109.
7. Barry, T. Johns Hopkins stays at the head of IS class. *Datamation,* January 15, 1988, 66.
8. Latour, B. and Woolgar, S. *Laboratory life: the social construction of scientific facts.* London: Sage, 1979.

9. Cronin, B. and Davenport, L. Libraries and the university value chain. *British Journal of Academic Librarianship*, 2(2), 1987, 85–90.
10. Davenport, L. and Cronin, B. Value added reselling and public domain data. *Electronic and Optical Publishing Review*, 7(1), 1987, 8–12.
11. Quoted in: Schwarzkopf, L. C. News from Washington. *Government Publications Review*, 16(5), 1989, 519–526.
12. Pearce, D. N. I. The assets of a nation. In Myers, J. (ed.). *Information and library services: policies and perspectives*. London: Aslib/IIS, 1990, 10–20.
13. Stephens, A. The application of life cycle costing in libraries. *British Journal of Academic Librarianship*, 3(2), 1988, 82–88.

3
VALUE ANALYSIS

Value Variables

In this chapter we explore several approaches to value. How to get more of it for money; where to look for it; how to measure it. Academic work in this area has focused on two primary areas: exchange value and value-in-use. We will examine the former in chapter 5; here our perspective is value-in-use.

Information only has value if it is appropriate to the task or situation in hand. An information manager must ensure that this is the case, but there are questions to be answered:

- How can you anticipate what will be of use?
- How do you assess the shelf life of what you have?
- What is an appropriate measure of value?
- What can you do to facilitate such measurement?
- How do you optimize your information base?

All of these questions are relevant to the management of information assets, the topic of the previous chapter. The area is, however, problematic, as users' concepts of information vary and their assessments of value may relate specifically to a variety of tasks in hand. In addition, the value of information to an individual or organization may be symbolic as well as practical, in which case different, possibly conflicting, parameters may apply.[1]

Practical and Symbolic Value

Some of the focal metaphors used in chapter one illustrate this point. Take *property*: its symbolic value may lie in the enhanced status conferred on the owner (Hyannisport or Belgravia are "good" addresses), in its heritage associations (the homestead; national monument; listed building), or exclusivity (vetting of would-be apartment owners in New York's upper East side to maintain quality; outstanding architectural features). Pragmatic or practical attributes also influence perceptions of value. These may have logistic implications, like downtown location or proximity to amenities (shops, leisure facilities, communications). Or site evaluation and selection may depend on strategic considerations: security (the importance of defensible space) or exploitable resources (the presence of mineral reserves).

Like property, information may have both practical and symbolic value. The Bill of Rights has symbolic value as a heritage document; its practical value as a *current* statement of acceptable and desirable individual liberties, however, may be debated, and frequently is in legislative fora. The symbolic value of a company or a brand name, as we indicated in the previous chapter, is often inflated above true asset value. The practical or pragmatic value of information, like that of property, lies in how easily it allows you to get from here to there in terms of decision making or direction (amenity value); how easily it allows you to exploit key resources (the equivalent of downtown location).

These logistic attributes are complemented by strategic factors: how defensible is this information in terms of patents, nondisclosure (security); how limited is its circulation (exclusivity) and what are the possibilities for wider or unforeseen exploitation (information reserves)? Other strategic factors influencing value are market demand (from the vendor's perspective), competition (who else is offering similar information at comparable prices?), proximity, or relatedness (can data sets be compared, combined?), integrity (can the accuracy of the information be guaranteed?), quality of construction (which might be important in software design, database structure, packaging).

We can apply the notions of symbolic and practical value to another of the key metaphors which we identified in chapter 1, *weaponry*. The flick knife in the hip pocket has a different value from the *skean dhu* in the kilt stocking. The former can offer practical defense from attack; the latter symbolizes the fighting spirit of those for whom highland dress was a military uniform.

The value of a weapon (literally, or metaphorically, from an information perspective) will depend on the relative advantage conferred. The information equivalent of a first, or preemptive strike is the patent, which creates a no-go zone around an idea or invention. A nuclear stockpile with IBM-delivery capability is a powerful military deterrent, just as sunk investment in a state-of-the-art information system can be a major entry barrier to a potential competitor. The comfort and protection afforded a ready arsenal are echoed in the sense of security provided by effective business intelligence or environmental scanning systems within organizations.

The *commodity* metaphor (which will be the focus of chapter 5) is of primary importance to the management of information in practical terms: commodities can be sold or bartered in a market-place or stockpiled to manipulate demand and inflate prices. But they can also be symbolically traded in forward markets by speculators.

Economic Goods

Economists classify goods in terms of attributes which reflect a consumer's experience. Search goods can be evaluated before they are acquired (in information terms these might be

off-the-shelf software and retailed hardware); the value of
experience goods is apparent only some time after acquisition
and early use (the case with a customized information system
or service), while the value of a hidden property good may not
be realized for some considerable time (a conference paper
may trigger an insight months after the event). These
categories are distinguished by the point in time at which
value is apparent, or a judgment is made. [see exhibit 3.1]

Value Typology

In exhibit 3.2 we describe seven types of value: these are not
mutually exclusive. Some can be expressed in book-keeping
terms (value-in-use; exchange value; insurable value). The
others reflect benefits which may be used to justify investments, but are not susceptible to standard accounting.

A repair manual is a simple example of how information
can have value-in-use. It allows you to do something you
could not do before, thus augmenting your technical skills.
Conceptual skills can be augmented in a similar way, where
value-in-use is reflected in transformed perceptions (fresh
perspectives). Comparative information refers to reconnais-

EXHIBIT 3.1

Information as a Commodity

SEARCH GOODS	EXPERIENCE GOODS	HIDDEN PROPERTY GOODS
Information Technology	Information Services	Information
Evaluate then acquire	Evaluate after acquisition	Epiphanic
Immediate assessment	Fixed period assessment	Open ended assessment

EXHIBIT 3.2
Types of Value

VALUE-IN-USE	Application (use manual to start car) Transformation (new perception; change gestalt) Comparison (avoid duplication; defend originality)
EXCHANGE VALUE	Price or equivalent (what you are willing to pay for information)
OPTION VALUE	Decision to use or not use at some future time
INSURABLE VALUE	Replacement costs (to rebuild database/archive)
LATENT VALUE	Unappreciated value (realized when circumstances/ perceptions change)
COVERT VALUE	Valuable because hidden (military/commercial intelligence)
INTEGRATIVE VALUE	Completeness of knowledge stock/set (pecuniary externalities)

sance activities (like patent searching) which establish the state-of-the-art and thus prevent duplication of research with the concomitant costs. In these examples value may be expressed in terms of time saved, or resources conserved. Both are quantifiable.

Exhibit 3.3 shows how difficult it is to achieve a single measure of value for information.[2] Even where you settle on one parameter like value-in-use, it is likely to be highly subjective. Exchange value is reflected in what the recipient is prepared to give for the information. That may be cash (for use of online services), sexual favors (Mata Hari), protection (offered by police to an informer), hospitality (lunch for gossip), or barter. You may give too much or too little; hindsight will tell.

The justification for sustained support of an information system or service might be based in part on its option value. In this case, current usage levels may be low, but the option to use at some future date is open to all members of the

EXHIBIT 3.3

Factors influencing perceptions of the value of information	
Evident costs	Information acquisition has visible and measurable costs in staff, equipment and purchases.
Uncertain return	Positive result of decisions are often not directly attributable to the availibility of the information on which they were based.
Long-term return	Evident benefits from information use tend to be long-term: expenses incurred in obtaining it are short-term.
Not directly productive	Information from databases is rarely used in production processes or contributes directly or measurably to production efficiency: it tends to be valuable in planning and research.
Overhead expense	Information services are regarded as an overhead and consequently are vulnerable to cost-cutting exercises.
Differential use	Relatively few people use information services directly; many have little personal contact with formal services.

[Source: Hayes & Erikson]

Reproduced from R. M. Hayes and T. Erickson, Added value as a function of purchases of information services. *Information Society*, 1(4), 1982, 307–338. Reprinted by permission of Hemisphere Publishing Corporation, a member of the Taylor & Francis Group.

organization, who may derive comfort (a valid psychological construct, but difficult to quantify) from the fact of its existence. In the case of public sector services, where information may be viewed as a public good, option value is important. It's October 17, 1989, in San Francisco, and the earthquake has put your communications, data, software and hardware out of commission. The main questions that occupy you are: "how much will it cost to reconfigure and rebuild?" and "what is the value to the business of the information system/service?" If the company has taken out an insurance policy on its systems/services it will be required to estimate replacement costs (for information content, as well as hardware). In this way, insurable value acts as a surrogate (albeit inflated) for exchange value and value-in-use.

The last three value categories (latent, covert, integrative) are not easily represented in terms of standard accounting practice. Latent value is, by definition, under-appreciated: it may be ascribed to information collected for one purpose whose significance proves to be greater in an alternative context[3], or it may be realized, where links are made between previously separate files. Think of a relational database, for example, which welds discrete customer files (product or account-based) into a multifaceted resource. This can yield fresh perspectives in response to queries based on different sets of attributes.

In the world of military and commercial espionage, the value of information lies in its official non-existence. Non-disclosure and restricted circulation are critical attributes. Covert information may in addition be of latent value. Take the case where total intelligence gathering on a particular community produces a resource capable of generating profiles of suspects (in the military context) or customers (in the civilian environment) far removed from the contexts in which the information was gathered.

Our last category is for information which functions as a coping stone, solves a puzzle, provokes a *gestalt,* or completes an individual's knowledge stock. In some cases, the import of the information may be latent; in others, its significance and effect may be immediately apparent. Such information may result in a new chemical compound or a definitive design that generates returns which greatly exceed the estimated value in relation to the original task in hand (pecuniary externalities).

Measures of Value

Various techniques have been used to measure the apparent value of information at both the macro and micro levels. A common approach is to explore the relationship between information and productivity. Results, however, are inconclusive.[4] In part, the problem stems from definitional uncertainty; in part from the differing perspectives employed; in part from the time horizon used.

The three-dimensional matrix in exhibit 3.4 is a framework for classification of research in this area. The *contexts* vary from sectoral, organizational and intra-organizational studies (at the level of the strategic business unit or line of business) to explorations of how specific individuals or groups use information in the workplace. Standard methods (*modes* in our exhibit) include cost-benefit analysis, econometric modelling and multivariate analysis, all of which involve input/output indicators.

The measures used in a typical cost-benefit or cost-effectiveness analysis (CBA) exercise will be local and specific, with benefits being expressed in terms of cost reductions, time saved or redeployed, or efficiency gains (saleforce or office automation projects are likely scenarios). In econometric modeling, the terms of an equation which describes a relationship between production, capital and labor, for example, are switched to produce an expression of productivity in terms of information and labor. Information resources are thus revealed as active factors in the production of goods and services.[5]

EXHIBIT 3.4

Value Analysis: Research Matrix

Context

Mode / Focus	Cost-benefit Analysis	Econometric Modelling	Multivariate Analysis	Behavioral	Normative
Macro-level					
Sectoral					
Organization					
SBU/LBO					
Individual					
Information Technology					
Information Services					
Information					

Multivariate analysis, in contrast, seeks to factor out the influence of information-related variables on business performance. What, in other words, is the relative impact of IT investment on profitability compared with other key variables (market share, fixed capital intensity, level of unionization, relative product quality)? In fact, there is no simple correlation between organizational spending on computers and either return on investment (ROI) or shareholder dividends.[6] Some factors *do* appear to be important: the alignment of IT investment with explicit business strategy, for example. As the overhead costs associated with these methodologies are high, the level of uptake is likely to be low. It may be that information investment will continue to be justified in terms of personal bias, "me-too-ism," or financial prestidigitation.

Behavioral/social anthropological and normative approaches have also been used. Case studies and anecdotal reporting characterize the first of these. The second provides benchmarks for expenditure (inter-firm comparisons; inter-sectoral norms and trends).

Expenditure is a way of trying to gauge the information intensity of organizations. Some common benchmarks in this context could be proportion of operational budget, turnover or pre-tax profit allocated to information sources, systems and services. An organization's total spending on information processing and handling is the sum of all direct and indirect expenditures on equipment (hardware, software, telecommunications), bought-in services and products, and information personnel. Many accountants disaggregate the IS (information systems) spending for a company or industry sector because it is highly visible, easy to determine[7] and may serve as a guide to the likely impact of information investment when used in conjunction with performance data on leaders and laggards.

Most difficult, perhaps, is trying to put a value on discrete quanta of information (the epiphanic effect noted in exhibit 3.1). As there is often no single metric of information, how do we define what is to be measured, given the impossibility of separating one quantum (assuming it could be isolated) and valuing it independently of all other inputs?

Structure and Value

Information can be assigned a value if it is used in a tightly structured and contained environment where protocols ensure that there is a match between what is sought and what is provided. Protocols might be reporting structures, standard classification, schemata, thesauri, data communication standards (X.400; X.25; OSI). Such structuring to some extent begs the question of the value of information, since protocols are designed to admit only material which conforms to agreed criteria. The implications of this are twofold: first, much information remains beyond the pale, unrecognized and therefore unexploitable; second, all information admitted into the structured environment must somehow be processed (formatted; edited; labeled; converted) and this entails an army of ancillaries or clerical and technical intermediaries who interface between raw material and users (an occasional source of dysfunction, as there is many a slip between cup and lip).

There is a range of contexts in which structure can facilitate the delivery of appropriate or valuable information. At the basic level, an information retrieval system matches input, via a controlled vocabulary or thesaurus, against content to ensure useful output in terms of either precision (specificity) or recall (scope). The value of output in such a case may be endorsed by the user, whose response conditions the system's assessment of what is required (query negotiation and relevance feedback). In more sophisticated systems, the retrieval process is based on clusters of textual elements which are held to represent meaning more accurately than simple keywords.[8] Moreover, intelligent front-ends or expert systems can assist with the identification of significant material in highly specific domains.[9]

The structured environment might be a specialist discipline, where what is admissable as evidence is strictly controlled. In a court of law, the value of a particular piece of information may be exactly defined, if it is a clinching quantum of circumstantial evidence, testimony or effective precedent. In scientific research, an item of information may confirm the identity of a substance or organism, where the attributes of an unknown entity are tested against known analogues (bacterial taxonomy, for example). In both these contexts, a particular quantum might assume great significance because it completed a set of associations. The *heurēka* phenomenon is, of course, common in the context of invention: "the essence of the concept of creativity is the fundamental notion 'aha!' which means a fresh and relevant association of thoughts, facts and ideas into a new pattern which has a significance overcoming the sum of the facts, hence leading to a synergetic effect."[10]

At the organizational level, the formal reporting structure of a large information system is intended to optimize the flow of valuable information. Effective communication will make sure that things get done in line with agreed business objectives: thus, strategy shapes structure. Choice of technology should be guided by the same principle.

If systems investment is premised on stated business objectives (increased market share; shorter lead times), and these are reflected in design, the contribution of information to performance should be clear. In every organization there are certain factors which are critical to successful performance, and these should condition the systems analysis process. Take the case of a company with the long-term goal of increasing market share. What sort of intelligence is needed? What sources need to be tapped . . . which competitors monitored? Who needs the information? A design which is driven by such questions will deliver appropriately focused information.

There is a danger, however, that such structures may ossify and that communication becomes ritualistic rather than adaptive. How can that structure be flexible enough to accommodate a change in focus or objectives? It is important that any system design should tolerate a degree of freedom in input and output. *Adaptive connectivity* is the term used by Beer[11], whose viable systems model uses cybernetic principles to ensure survival across changing circumstance. In its simplest form, his model offers a technique for regulating stimuli and response between three basic building blocks (environment, operations and management); the prerequisite of successful interaction is "requisite variety," as no model or systems design can do justice to what it models unless it is at least as complex as the reality it represents.

The selection of appropriate variables for understanding or modeling an organization is a prerequisite of effective system design. Tradeoffs must always be made between what is technically feasible (something that works) and what constitutes an adequate representation of information transfer and use in the context being modeled (something that allows the whole story to be told). Designs that work tend to be simple; organizational communication tends to complexity, as it reflects social and political purposes whose significance may often be ambivalent or covert.[12] In many cases it has been easier to ignore such implications and treat information as potentially valuable only in crisply defined contexts.

Information may be seen as valuable where it supports a case, in any context. Advocacy is as necessary in the boardroom as the courtroom, and useful information is that which can be construed as supporting evidence or what influences the outcome of a decision. Persuasion goes beyond facts at fingertips: successful rhetoric is based in part on knowing your audience. The information input to successful case presentation will include effective intelligence (what we termed street information in chapter 1), and much of this lies outside the world of structured information.

Decision Support

Some writers consider that value can only be isolated in the specific context of decision support, where this process is modeled as a decision tree whose alternatives are assessed as desirable or not on the basis of probable outcome. Case study analysis indicates that the methodology applied to information investment is unwieldly and carries a considerable overhead.[13] Many decision support systems (DSS) do not take soft factors into account and assume that cases are won on the basis of rational assessment of a comprehensive set of alternatives (synoptic rationality). In practice, decisions may be grounded in imperfect information (an arbitrary patchwork of elements or disjointed incrementalism).[14]

In some cases, the information input is not apparent until after the event, to justify a decision based on gut reaction. As a general rule, the inputs to a gut reaction will have been ingested so long ago that they are unrecognizable. In the physical sense they are metabolized by the system that consumed them, and they no longer have a separate identity. Likewise, the information which colors a gut reaction is no longer recognizable; it has been absorbed, digested, embedded in a background of social and political assumptions, and transformed into intuition. In such cases, the processes of locating, accessing and evaluating information are largely subconscious.

Inventories and Maps

At the level of the organization, however, the allocation of information resources must be transparent to avoid wastage, to demonstrate distributive justice and to achieve the best fit between task and technology. The first step is mapping what is required against what is available. Horton[15] has developed a simple methodology for mapping an organization's information resource base, which goes beyond box counting. The approach is very much that of overhead value analysis (ranking supplier estimates of costs against receiver value judgments), and there is little emphasis on information as a lever of opportunity. His basic unit is a composite of information sources, systems and services. The role of the information manager is to make an inventory of these information resource entities (IREs), determine the criteria for recognizing IREs, classify existing resources, determine associated costs and rank the IREs in terms of perceived value. The steps involved may be formalized as follows:

- survey/produce inventory
- measure costs and assess value
- analyze and review both costs and values
- identify corporate IREs and assess resource strengths and weaknesses

An organization's IREs will emerge from a detailed analysis of three areas:

- sources (the place, store or person from which information can be obtained, either internal or external)
- services (activities which are helpful in acquiring, processing or transmitting information)
- systems (a structured and integrated series of processes for handling information or data)

The labeling of different IREs will depend on the level of aggregation of the analysis and on the context of the survey. For example, some individuals may view a library as a source, others as a service. The process of location, identification, classification and review, which involves discussions with three key constituencies, information users, information handlers and information suppliers, is summarized in a flow chart. The data gathered from such an exercise can be mapped in one of two ways. The first generates a matrix setting information resource (source, system, service) against organizational unit (the preferred level may be division, department or unit). The resultant worksheet is, in effect, a pointillistic picture of who uses and who supplies/produces which IREs in the organization.

Horton also suggests that the information resources of an organization may be literally mapped in a bounded space, the north/south coordinates of which are functions (the flows, actions or movements needed for handling information) and holdings (the static record/form in which information is held); the east/west dimensions of the map are content/media and conduit.[16] A similar approach to mapping the information industry was taken at Harvard by McLaughlin and Antonoff[17] in the early 1980s using comparable coordinates. Other information resource maps are based on coordinates which reflect organizational performance rather than attributes of the resource themselves: we discuss some of these in chapter 4.

What distinguishes a map from an inventory? Maps perform two basic functions: they place entities in relation to one another, vertically and laterally; and they supply coordinates which allow the user to negotiate reality. Horton allows you to rank IREs, but as a tool for strategic orientation the approach has its limitations, though it does offer a wide-angled snapshot of resource distribution and intensity [see exhibit 3.5]. Where, however, appropriate criteria (the coordinates of the map; root definition of IREs) are agreed, such "infomaps" could be used to provide inter-firm and inter-sectoral profiles. These, by providing benchmarks, could guide a company's information investment strategy, by indicating where resources should be deployed to maintain a competitive position.

Value Engineering

Horton invokes the work of Bedell[18] to provide an evaluative framework for IREs, the basis of which is a score card. There are three simple stages in his methodology:

- rate the effectiveness with which the IRE supports the activity or activities it was designed to support
- rate the strategic importance of the IRE in the conduct of this activity
- rate the strategic importance to the organization of the activity supported

An IRE is deemed effective if it meets pre-defined information requirements, is functionally effective and technically adequate within the context of the company activity it supports. Information resource entities can be ranked in terms of four indicative indexes:

- the RE Index—resource effectiveness index
- the IA Index—importance to activity index

EXHIBIT 3.5

Corporate Information Map
for
Mining/Minerals Company

Media/Conduit →

Content →

Functions →

Functions

Holding →

Holding

Media/Conduit

Media/Conduit

Mail Service (37)
Courier Services (8)
Telex system (73)
Microform Reader-Printers (40)
Photocopiers (56)

Telephone System (72)

Computer Systems (7)

Drafting Service (10)
Computer Service B (6)
Geographic Info System (27)
Computer Graphics Terminals (4)

Drafting System (11)
Word Processors (74)

Current Awareness Service (9)
Minerals Literature Service (42)
Federal Library Service (22)

Online Database Service A (50)
Online Database Service B (51)
Online Database Service C (52)

National Geoscience Bibliographic System (49)

Image Analysis System (32)
Magnetic Data Analysis System (36)
Geochemical Data Analysis System (25)

Remote Sensing Data Analysis Service (62)
Geological Interpretation Service (28)

Aerial Photography Service (1)

Bibliographic Data (3)
Exploration Reports Index (18)
Remote Sensing Biblio Database (60)

Drill-Log Data System (13)
Laboratory Data Service (34)

Image Analysis Slide Catalogue (31)
Minerals Exhibit Catalogue (45)

Laboratory Analysis System (33)
Sample Data Management System (65)

Resource Evaluation Service (64)
Computer Service A (5)

Geophysical Survey Index (2)
Exploration Well Index (19)
Petroleum Permit Index (53)
Exploration Service B (15)

Prospects Reporting System (59)

Field Data Coding System (23)
Geochem Sampling System (26)
Prospects Coding System (57)

Research Information Service (63)
Technical Info Service (71)

Federal Geoscience Agency (20)
State Geoscience Agency A (66)
State Geoscience Agency B (67)
State Geoscience Agency C (68)
State Geoscience Agency D (69)
State Geoscience Agency E (70)

Mineral Deposit Database Service (41)
Minerals Info And Data Service (46)

Geochemical Data (24)
Geophysical Dat (30)
Remote Sensing Data (61)

Federal Geoscience Databases (21)

Exploration Info Service C (16)

Geological Sample Data (29)
Drill-Log & Assay Data (12)

Exploration Info Service A (14)

Petroleum Well Data Service (55)
Prospects Data (50)
Mineral Lease Data (43)

Mining Information (47)
Petroleum Information (54)

Management Dept (48)

Library Service (35)

Mineral Lease Data Service (44)

Maps & Charts (39)

Exploration Reports (17)

Management Info (38)

Reproduced from F. W. Horton, Mapping corporate information resources. *International Journal of Information Management*, 8, 1988, 249–254. Reprinted by permission of Butterworth Scientific Ltd.

- the IO Index—importance to the organization index
- the Value Index—the product of the previous three

The relative position of resource entities will be apparent, as the rating scheme reflects values across the entire organization. The methodology has its limitations. The first procedural weakness is the distortion which occurs when one of the index scores is zero, as this results in a row multiple (the Value Index) with a value of zero. The second is the subjectivity of the scoring process, which restricts its worth to local evaluations of resources.

Subjective Accounting

As for source information in a research and development environment, it may be possible to convert subjective evaluations of the "this information was extremely useful" kind into monetary (or monetary equivalent) statements of value-in-use. In a series of studies, King Research[19] has attempted to put a bottom-line value on information. If we assume that the cost of providing an in-company information service averages out at $1,000 per annum per professional/managerial employee, the net return on investment (ROI) can fall in the range 4.5:1 to 11.5:1 [see exhibit 3.6]. How are these figures arrived at? Quite simply: (a) by asking users (scientists, engineers, managers) to say how much they would be prepared to pay for the information they currently use; (b) by calculating what it would cost (time converted into dollars on the basis of known salary levels) to acquire the information elsewhere; and (c) by itemizing benefits which would otherwise have been lost (for instance: reading a technical report may mean that laboratory experiments are not repeated, thus time and materials are saved [see exhibit 3.7]). The message is clear: as far as the seek-and-find aspect of information provision is concerned, if users are left to fend for themselves, costs go up and value goes down.

EXHIBIT 3.6
Value Quantification

Value Perspective	Average value per professional	ROI
Willingness to pay	$4, 500	4.5:1
Additional cost to use alternative sources	$3, 800	3.8:1
Lost benefits	$11,500	11.5:1

Reproduced from D. W. King and J.-M. Griffiths, The information advantage. In: B. Cronin and N. Tudor-Silovic (eds.), *Information resource management: concepts, strategies, applications.* London: Taylor Graham, 1989, pp. 56–68. Reprinted by permission of Taylor Graham.

But caution is advised: what individuals *say* and what they *do* are quite different things (the experimental/halo effect). Second, the amount users *say* they are willing to pay is a hypothetical expression of exchange, *not* consequential value. Third, this approach makes assumptions about the appropriateness of the activities performed by the survey population, which may be open to question. The value perspective used is that of the individual manager/researcher, not the parent/ funding body (task-related, not strategic). The two may not always be aligned.

Time Savings Times Salary

A related approach (the hedonic wage model) has been used by Sassone and Schwarz[20] to measure the return on investment in office automation (OA). A major OA project

EXHIBIT 3.7

Savings from Readings of Technical Reports

Report topic	$ Value of time saved	$ value of supplies saved	How time saved
Highway vehicle systems	1,600		did not have to search for materials
Tritium recovery from fusion blankets	500		non-repetition of results
Decommissioning handbook	10,000+		shortened planning process
Wood gasification	2,000	2,000+	did not have to conduct experiments
Thermal analysis of spirogel microspheres	200	20,000+	did not have to prepare and conduct experiments

Derived from D. W. King et al., The value of the energy data base. Report to the Department of Energy. Rockville, MD: King Research/Department of Energy, 1982.

will alter the composition of a job and associated task responsibilities. It typically generates two kinds of benefits:

- efficiency gains (shortens the time to complete a task, or allows more to be accomplished in a given time)
- work restructuring (increases effectiveness which is not measured by conventional cost justification and productivity criteria)

In any organization, the worth of workers is the weighted value of the activities they perform. The first step is to identify the main employee classifications and activities performed: a simplified taxonomy would be professional (high level; high value; high cost), clerical and unproductive. Step two involves logging work activity for a representative, stratified sample of employees; step three requires the collection of data on salary levels, fringe benefits, overtime, vacation periods, etc. If there is a quantified post-installation shift to higher level work (a net gain of 100 hours, say), you can calculate the monetary value of the gain (ROI) at the implicit value rate.

This approach (as with the King studies) has its limitations. Measurable value restructuring may occur: you may be spending 15 percent more of your time on managerial tasks (in planning/policy meetings) but it does not necessarily follow that you are being proportionately more *effective* in attaining organizational objectives. Suppose, however, you use this 15 percent with unprecedented effectiveness; the actual benefits to the company could be much greater than simple adjusted value. It is an easy matter to estimate the opportunity cost of an OA installation (how else could the time and money have been spent?); it is much more difficult to foresee the opportunities which might emerge in the wake of implementation. Move beyond OA to more sophisticated IS investments and the scope for unexpected innovation (and surprise value) grows. The wider the window of opportunity, the narrower the relevance of traditional cost-benefit analysis.[21]

A limitation of the Horton/Bedell approach is the focus on static information entities. Though Horton recommends that soft factors should be taken into account, his methodology does not embrace the idea of organizations as "discourses, cultures, tribes, political battlegrounds, quasi-families, or communication and task networks."[22] In summary, inventory control is proffered as a tool of management, rather than analysis of information flow.

Information Flows

As a basic case, consider a unit in a government department responsible for the production and distribution of quarterly trade statistics. In Horton's terms these data sets might constitute one IRE in the department's overall inventory. We would know who used it and how they ranked it, but little or nothing about the factors influencing its routing and use throughout the organization. The Horton/Bedell approach might be extended and the IRE tracked using the kind of schematic featured in exhibit 3.8. This records the flow of information from department 0/1 (the source) to various nodes in other departments, where the flow may terminate or be switched, either to another unit within that department, or to a different department. The objective is to chart the direction and pace of information diffusion, and to identify structural blockages, wastage, duplication and inefficiencies in the system.

In our illustration there is a direct flow from source to final recipient (4/5), but the route from source to a trinity of recipients in department 3/4 is twice mediated. Need that be the case? The isolate in department 0/1 is not on the circulation list: should he be? In department 2/3 there is duplication of effort, as two nodes are exchanging the same message received from a superordinate. Why is that happening? In department 4/5 the ultimate node receives the same message from two sources. Again, duplication of effort.

EXHIBIT 3.8

Inter Unit / Department Value Chain

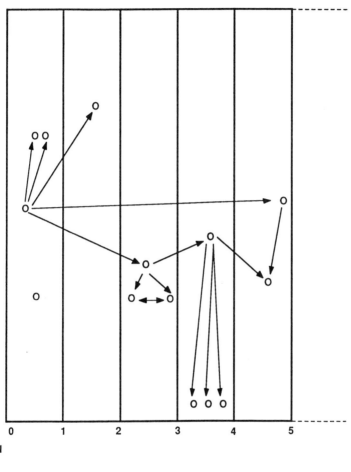

0 1 2 3 4 5

ORIGIN

INFORMATION FLOW

The purpose of the exercise is to provide answers to a number of basic questions:

- What kinds and volume of information are flowing in the system? At what level of aggregation: full trade statistics, summary tables, selected data sets?
- When is the information dispatched from the source and when does it reach user departments?
- What is the extent of information float? Where are the blockages in the distribution chain, and what/who causes them?
- Why is the information gathered and distributed in the first place? Do supplier and receiver departments agree on the reasons?
- What happens to the information when it leaves the source department? Is it ignored, filed, acted on, stored, transformed, disposed of, reformatted, combined with other information?
- Is the information of value (essential; nice-to-have; of little or no use)?
- What costs are associated with the production and use chain?
- Are the statistics being distributed in the most appropriate form of subsequent local processing?
- Is there a market for the data outside government? If so, has value-added reselling been considered?

The aggregate costs of producing quarterly trade data may be minuscule in the context of the department's or government's information-related expenditures, but the approach advocated here, and schematized in exhibit 3.9, could be applied to all key activities (and associated IREs) carried out in a specific department, *or* across all government departments. Given the information-intensive nature of public administration, value analysis exercises of this kind, which juxtapose demand and supply side variables, can result in

EXHIBIT 3. 9

Cost and Value Tracking Methodology

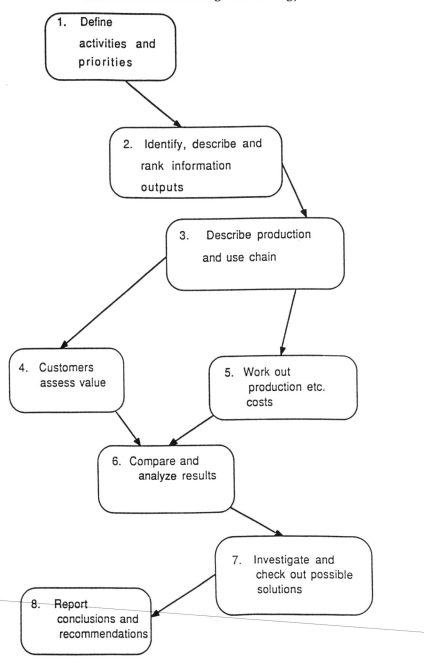

more efficient, economic and effective information management.[23]

Speech Acts and Transactions

We now look at approaches which take a holistic view of information in organizations; our first focus is conversation. Exhibit 3.8 showed how information flow may be prone to dysfunction, with loose ends and dead ends a cause of value loss. How can you avoid such problems? By limiting the degrees of freedom of exchange in the system, and by sending information only to those who are "contractually" committed to acting on it, in other words, by structuring information flow along lines which ensure its effectiveness. Suppose we reconceptualize an organization as a complex of markets and conversations (between individuals within and across departmental units); management becomes the art of initiating, monitoring and coordinating such exchanges.

The understanding of what an information system really does, requires an appreciation of the socio-political context in which it is designed, built, purchased, installed and used. Systems can be seen as "despatchers of heuristics, commitments and promises which streamline the negotiation process embedded in any exchange."[24] The organization of work in an office, for instance, can be deconstructed into a series of more or less formally stated commitments. These are manifest in conversational exchanges which in turn can be reduced to a few simple building blocks: Searle[25] has divided speech acts into five basic types [see exhibit 3.10]. His formalized representation of communication (assertives, directives, commissives, expressives, declaratives) provides the foundation elements for Winograd and Flores' Coordinator™ Workgroup Productivity System.

This aims "to provide a ready-to-hand tool that operates in the domain of conversations for action." Winograd and Flores describe speech acts in terms of dyads:

- request/promise
- offer/acceptance
- report/acknowledge

The Coordinator software *commits* members of an organization to participate. It is the software instantiation of a "gentleman's agreement" ("my word is my bond"). A major drawback of e-mail systems is the backlog of ignored and unanswered messages. With the Coordinator software, the sender can transmit a message with a specific respond-by date, knowing that the rules of engagement call for an explicit statement of recipient intent (promise; renege; assert). The frustrations and inefficiencies of conventional computer messaging need no longer apply, as the permissive world of

EXHIBIT 3.10
Searle's Five Basic Communication Types

* ASSERTIVES ... commit the speaker to the truth of a proposition

* DIRECTIVES ... attempt to get the hearer to do something

* COMMISSIVES ... commit the speaker to some future course of action

* EXPRESSIVES ... indicate the psychological response to a state of affairs (e.g. apology; praise)

* DECLARATIVES ... bring about a correspondence between propositional content and reality (e.g. pronouncing a couple man and wife)

Derived from J. R. Searle, Expression and meaning: studies in the theory of speech acts. Cambridge: Cambridge University Press, 1979.

conventional electronic mail is replaced by regulated discourse [see exhibit 3.11].

What are the benefits of this kind of approach? Its designers claim that it reduces information float; avoids redundancy; improves consignment tracking (has A answered B's request by the agreed date?), improves time management, and encourages prioritization. Most of these benefits can be expressed in monetary equivalent terms using the conversion techniques suggested by King and others. Conversations also take place *between* organizations, where suppliers commit themselves to a delivery date, price and quality level. Such exchanges are the basis of existing electronic data interchange (EDI) systems which have produced demonstrable and considerable savings for participating companies.

The Coordinator, which is in some ways an analogue of an EDI system, may reasonably be expected to generate similar measurable benefits. Users, however, of a pilot system at Pacific Bell described it as "worse than a lobotomized file clerk": for some it is too reductionist and fails to take account of interpretive understanding or the feeling states of individuals.[26]

Strategic Value

The techniques we have discussed reflect value-in-use, expressed directly (problem solved) or in terms of surrogate benefits (measured in units that can be costed, like hours saved at a specific wage rate or resources not consumed) and this allows them to appear on the balance sheet. Many of the benefits which arise from information investment (new business opportunities; new perspectives; innovations; inventions) are open-ended and not amenable to cost-accounting. Economists and accountants are actively seeking workable alternatives to cost-benefit analysis.

These may be bundled under the label strategic value analysis, which is based on the following premises:

EXHIBIT 3.11

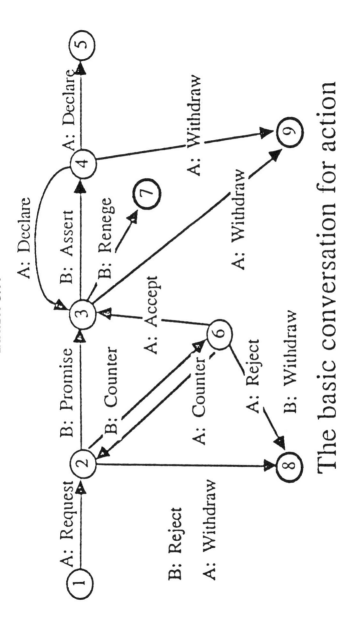

The basic conversation for action

- information and information technology are inseparable (the holistic approach)
- benefits need to be seen in terms of competitive advantage (affecting change in industry structure, or the rules of the game), not merely cost-cutting
- information investments often entail new, untried or unprecedented applications whose impacts cannot be predicted with accuracy
- investment decisions are based on an assessment of business, technical and economic viability
- there must be tight fit between business strategy and IT strategy
- risk aversion may be a liability (greenfield situations call for investor nerve)
- value may be compound

The Value Chain

A useful tool for assessing the strategic value of information has been developed by Porter.[27] In discussing value he does not distinguish information and information technology. This allows him to identify benefits from information investment at any level of company activity. He classifies the internal activities of an enterprise into nine specific groups. Five of these are primary activities dealing with raw material acquisition, production, marketing and delivery of a product; in other words in the line activities of the business. The remaining four are support or backbone activities such as human resources management [see exhibit 3.12].

The four support activities may be seen as overhead activities, which add cost. Porter suggests that their value can be expressed in terms of relative cost savings or increased productivity using the terms of conventional accounting, but a new accounting paradigm is required for his five primary activities.

He presents these as a chain: "The value chain disaggre-

EXHIBIT 3.12

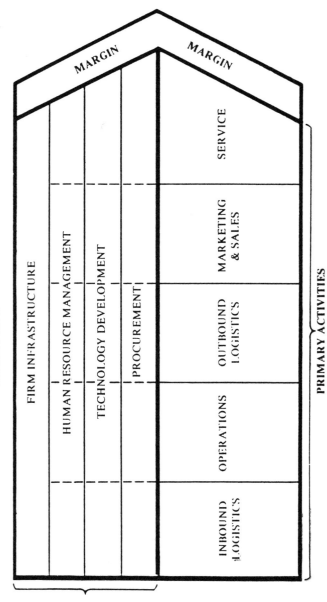

gates a firm into its strategically relevant activities in order to understand the behavior of costs and the existing and potential sources of differentiation. A firm gains competitive advantage by performing these strategically important activities more cheaply or better than its competitors." Information adds value to primary activities by being attached to the product itself, or by changing the ways in which it is produced and delivered to customers. Differentiation can result from the piggy-backing of a technological enhancement onto a service or product; such bundling may happen at any stage of the distribution/marketing/support process. Otis Elevator has gained competitive edge in after-sales by seeing service as an *information* problem; one solution has been to install flight recording devices in its lifts, which can detail the cause of malfunctions, otherwise often inaccurately reported after the event.

By unearthing value within primary activities at the line of business (LOB) level, Porter's model transforms the scope of strategic information management, which will no longer be an ancillary activity or left in the hands of a separate task force. The primary activities which allow the corporation or organization to be seen as interlocked functional elements, also allow it to be conceptualized as a network of intelligence units monitoring internal and external environments.

The strategic importance of IT will vary across companies and industry sectors, and its likely impacts can be assessed in terms of four critical factors:

- information intensity (a feature of companies with many products, multi-stage production and a broad range of suppliers and distributors)
- role of IT in industry structure (the conduct of business in certain sectors, like banking and air travel, may be transformed)
- potential of IT to create competitive advantage (improved efficiency allows you to pare back costs and become price competitive)

- potential of IT to spawn new businesses (a company data base becomes the basis of commercial information service)

These four factors should lead to an action plan which allows an organization to capitalize on IT investments.

Porter's model can be used outside the corporate environment, as a management tool in local government, for example, or higher education.[28] Exhibit 3.13 is our analysis of how a U.K. university might apply Porter's Value Chain to unlock value in the five primary activities.

Parker and Benson[29] provide a more detailed campus model, along with other case scenarios. They use these to demonstrate a new approach to value analysis, or information economics, based on their perception of the compound value which emerges from linkages across segments of the value chain. The resultant multi-dimensional investment analysis model combines traditional CBA with new mechanisms for risk and innovation analysis. They use Porter's value chain as the basis of a novel accounting lexicon, which includes value *restructuring,* value *linking,* and value *acceleration.*

Value linking and value acceleration analysis are techniques to assess how value can be compounded, as benefits from one department spill over into other departments: think of a ripple effect *(linking).* Where information technology *accelerates* the delivery of products and services (computer integrated manufacture; online stock market price information), it also *accelerates* rewards or has a measurable effect on the bottom line. And we have already mentioned the case where value is realized through *restructuring* of employee or departmental efforts from lower to higher value activities (the hedonic model described by Sassone and Schwarz). The value chain is flexible. It need not describe self-contained institutions, and may be used to model relationships in a large vertically integrated enterprise, a holding company, a cooperative or a loose confederation of small independents. Whatever the configuration, the model is premised on linkages between information sources, systems and services.

EXHIBIT 3.13

	IN-BOUND LOGISTICS	OPERATIONS	OUT-BOUND LOGISTICS	MARKETING & SALES	SERVICE
PEOPLE	Prospecting	Processing	Placement	Promotion	Post-experience provision
INFORMATION	Input	Integration	Intelligence	Infusion	Impact assessment
MANAGEMENT	Materials	Manipulation	Maximization	Marketing	Mega-marketing

UNIVERSITY VALUE CHAIN: PIM MODEL

Filters and Fans

We have indicated some of the problems which attach to the evaluation of information, and have suggested approaches, none of them optimal, and many of them over-specific. Until recently, the solution was thought to be structure, which allows defined objectives (fast and accurate retrieval; reduced information float, or whatever) to be reflected in information design (via grouping, normalizing or optimal routing) at the level of the data set or the larger corporate information universe. In many cases, the operational benefits delivered by structured systems are precisely what managers need for the situation in hand. But to regard these as the sum of the benefits offered by information is myopic.

Structure as solution generates its own problems. It involves selection, and this means that potentially valuable material may be left out (the stuff that has latent, option or integrative value). The predominant metaphor of effective information use in the classic organization is the *filter* or funnel; a problem solver converges on a solution by discarding inappropriate evidence. We would like to suggest the *fan* as an equally appropriate managerial metaphor, or description of the widening of opportunity and perspective which results from free-range information gathering in the widest possible universe. Information in such a context will "allow us to move in innumerable ways," to paraphrase Simon.[30] It will be an agent of divergence and will generate alternatives, not restrict them.

Connection Engineering

A cluster of technologies has emerged which are based on the idea of highly interconnected trapping of information, a supposed analogue of the associative mechanism of the brain. These currently travel under a range of labels (hypertext, interactive multimedia in the publishing arena; neural nets and hypercubes in the domain of information processing). Their common design premise is a web or matrix of linked nodes, where intelligent traffic protocols allow superspeed processing of vast volumes of information. The frame of reference of such systems is orders of magnitude greater than what was previously possible.

Such systems are veritable technologies of abundance; restriction of information to accommodate the limitations of the processing machine is a thing of the past. Computer systems have traditionally added value to information in structured situations. Technology can now augment unstructured, serendipitous, browsing and grazing activities and facilitate the lateral leaps which characterize creativity. The expansion of the human capacity to model, and the development of shared and navigable frames of reference are serious management issues, reflected in questions like the following:

- what promises innovation?
- can it be fostered?
- how can we see things as others see them?
- how can we be sure that our models are accurate?
- how can we open up our referential base?

We examine two developments in detail, hypertext and connectionist machines, which address these issues in complementary ways. The first, hypertext, is a generic for a cluster of technologies for input, assembly, access, storage and retrieval which handle material, static or dynamic, in any medium, fixed or temporal. In such systems, texts (the term is not restricted to written material and refers to anything which has an owner on the system) are understood and handled as aggregates of elements of arbitrary length. These are joined by links to form a sequence, and the order may be specified by either producer (this results in the text as written) or user (the text as read); the two need not be the same.

The basic premise of hypertext is freedom of movement,

and users may choose to intercept the text by including their own glosses, comments or suggestions, or requests for information. Most conventional databases offer no clues about the origins and dependencies of documents, which at present are tracked only in terms of historical usage, a rough encoding of their content, or searches for particular words. With hypertext we have access to, and reworking of, layered document sets: the text-as-was at any given date can be reactivated or re-assembled from its appropriate fragments.[31]

Lateral Linking and Lateral Thinking

Hypertext can add value to the modeling process by allowing substrata to be explored, and by trapping the input which lies behind the selected variables. In the context of problem solving, backward (starting from the present) and forward (starting from some historical point) exploration of supporting documents is possible. Decisions, designs, reports (and other products of meetings) can be scrutinized; key or controversial points can be traced back and no stone need be left unturned (provided the evidence has been recorded) in the search for total accountability. Alternatives can be sustained, or resurrected right through a design or decision-making process, and managers need no longer stick with the wrong or inappropriate course simply to vindicate investment.

The staple information diet of most managers lies outside the structured environment. Decisions may be supported by structured information, but they are grounded in unstructured stimuli; reports from the front line (the field salesforce, for example), gossip. This type of material often carries more detail than formal (structured) systems, but there are still constraints on its exploitation; it is locked inside the manager's head, or diffusion is limited to a personal circle of contacts, and linkages cannot always be openly acknowledged, as many reporting structures do not admit verbal or informal evidence. Hypertext offers a way of loosening up structured information to accommodate extraneous comment, and to admit linkages across the augmented base.

Gestalt switches, changes in the perception of patterns which allow us to interpret a situation or a set of facts in a new way, emerge from the admission of alternatives, and can be encouraged by looking beyond closed sets or logically related non-interactive groups (of texts or people). Swanson's[32] comments on "postmature" literature, whose latent value is only apparent when an individual associates it with some latter-day frame of reference, can be applied to any textual mechanism which permits links to join material across the boundaries of predefined sets (the canning process). *Gestalt* need not involve a *heurēka* experience: a more protracted process of apprenticeship can be just as effective. A novice can follow the spoor of a traveler as he or she traverses an information set (such facilities are offered in commercial hypertext products and their value in training is obvious) and basic tracking can be supplemented with advice on how to behave and with whom to communicate in a specific domain to provide what is a virtual internship.[33]

What sort of value attaches to hypertextured information? It offers *value-as-used,* as distinct from *value-in-use,* as the links made to nodes or items can be qualified (in terms of corroboration or dissent), and audited (to provide a genealogy or archaeology of the sort we have described). The value of creativity, conceptual sharing and access to a wide evidential base can be expressed in both hard terms (reduced training costs) and soft terms (adaptiveness, consensus, trust). There is likely to be resistance to developments which break both cultural and procedural traditions, and advocates of liberation technology may be advised to stress hard benefits, rather than offer conflicting behavioral norms.

Hypertext allows the usable information universe to be expanded, by removing the barriers to cross-exploitation. Connectionist machines expand this universe by processing massively in parallel: the eponymous commercial version at MIT has 64,000 units working as a virtual network, customized for the problem of the moment, each one of which can process one element of a task. Problems need no longer be reduced to manageable proportions for the purposes of approximate modeling, what one designer calls "adding layers of artificiality." Take the case of an open-ended request for information, which resembles something that tickled your intellect. You place one text from your base on each processor: "The one you've got says, 'Here's what I'm like,' and everybody looks at that and says, 'How much am I like that?' and they order themselves in the order of how much they are like the other article. That whole operation takes fractions of a second for tens of thousands of articles."[34]

The trellis machine proposes something similar. A prototype for medical information has been developed to provide an information filter which sorts out interesting patterns from records of many similar objects or events. Full details on a patient's bodily condition (heart rate, blood pressure, temperature) are recorded; the system relates these to the patient's general condition by looking for trends and exceptions in the data. These in turn are scanned in a search for diagnoses. The system is self-referential. At each stage data flow upward from level to level through the connections in the trellis and interpretations are continuously revised. What is the value of such a system? Its designers claim that it can transform wasted data into information by addressing "the same basic question—'What's going on here?'—at many levels of detail."[35]

All of the current arenas of information management (design, collaborative work, multimedia, simulation, documentation) come within the scope of parallel machines. Each of the processors can replicate (and soon will be able to improve on) its genetic inheritance, and each machine will function as a miniature ecosystem where new forms emerge through evolutionary processes like those of the big world. Tricks and tropes and topics will emerge which are initiatives

EXHIBIT 3.14

Lateral Linking

CONSTRAINTS	PROMOTERS
Excessive structure	Hospitable, loose structure
Preconceptions	Open mind
Specialization	Generalist approach
Isolation	Networks
Sclerosis	Suppleness
Culture-bound	Maverick nature
Stupidity	Intelligence
Impermeability	Porosity
Convergence	Divergence
Inflexible technology	Flexible technology
Narrow outlook	Broadcatching

from the system, and human/computer interaction may assume new dimensions, with humans teased and challenged by their machines.

Just as interesting from the management point of view are the implications for human/human interaction. Connection engineering (we use the term to cover both hypertextual links and the virtual network of processors in the Connection Machine) will enhance the sharing of percepts and concepts, and attenuate misunderstanding.

In exhibit 3.14 we list some factors which promote and inhibit lateralism or connectivity; the "promoters" constitute an organizational utopia; if this is a recipe for success, why is it not more prevalent? Why do people continue to trade privately and discreetly? Why do they share selectively? The problem is competition, the subject of the next chapter.

References

1. Feldman, M. S. and March, J. G. Information in organizations as signal and symbol. *Administrative Science Quarterly*, 26, 1981,

171–186. See also: Repo, A. J. *Approach to the value of information: effectiveness and productivity of information use in research work.* Espoo: Technical Research Centre of Finland, 1989.

2. Hayes, R. M. and Erickson, T. Added value as function of purchases of information services, *Information Society,* 1(4), 1982, 307–338.
3. Davenport, E. and Cronin, B. Hypertext and the conduct of science. *Journal of Documentation,* 46(3), 1990, 175–192.
4. Cronin, B. and Gudim, M. Information and productivity: a review of research. *International Journal of Information Management,* 6(2), 1986, 85–101.
5. Hayes, R. M. Information and productivity. *IRCHIE Bulletin,* 6 (1–2), 1980, 20–35.
6. Strassmann, P. A. *Information technology and organizations.* London: Department of Industry/Rank Xerox, 1983.
7. See the *Datamation 100,* a sectoral review of information systems spending, produced annually by *Datamation.*
8. Willett, P. (ed.). Introduction to: *Document retrieval systems.* London: Taylor Graham, 1988.
9. Wormell, I. (ed.). *Knowledge engineering: expert systems and information retrieval.* London: Taylor Graham, 1987.
10. Quoted in: Purica, I. I. Creativity, intelligence and synergetic processes in the development of science. *Scientometrics,* 13 (1–2), 1988, 11–24.
11. Beer, S. *Diagnosing the system for organizations.* Chichester, Eng.: Wiley, 1985.
12. Checkland, P. B. Information systems and systems thinking: time to unite? *International Journal of Information Management,* 8(4), 1988, 239–248.
13. Carter, M. P. The valuing of information. Part I: the Bayesian approach. *Journal of Information Science,* 10(1), 1985, 1–9.
14. Lindblom, C. E. *The policy-making process.* Englewood Cliffs, NJ: Prentice-Hall, 1968.
15. Burk, C. F. and Horton, F. W. *Infomap: the complete guide to discovering corporate information resources.* Englewood Cliffs, NJ: Prentice-Hall, 1988.
16. Burk and Horton, *op.cit.*
17. McLaughlin, J. F. and Antonoff, A. L. *Mapping the information business.* Cambridge, MA: Program on Information Resources Policy, Harvard University, 1986.
18. Bedell, E. F. *The computer solution: strategies for success in the information age.* Homewood, IL: Dow Jones-Irwin, 1985.

19. King, D. W. et al. *The value of the energy data base.* Report submitted to the Department of Energy. Rockville, MD: King Research/Department of Energy, 1982.
20. Sassone, P. G. and Schwarz, H. P. Cost justifying OA. *Datamation,* 16 February 1986, 83–88.
21. Sassone, P. G. Cost benefit analysis of information systems: a survey of methodologies. *ACM SIGOIS Bulletin,* 9(2 & 3), 1988, 126–131.
22. Checkland, *op. cit.*
23. Sangway, D. Government approach to information management. *Aslib Proceedings,* 41(5), 1989, 179–187.
24. Ciborra, C. U. Research agenda for a transaction cost approach to information systems. In Boland, R. J. and Hirschheim, R. A. *Critical issues in information systems research.* Chichester, Eng.: Wiley, 1987, 253–274.
25. Searle, J. R. *Expression and meaning: studies in the theory of speech acts.* Cambridge: Cambridge University Press, 1979.
26. Flores, F. et al. Computer systems and the design of organizational interaction. *ACM Transactions on Office Information Systems,* 6(2) 1988, 153–172. For a user view see: Carasik, R. P. and Grantham, C. E. A case study of CSCW in a dispersed organization. In Soloway, E. et al. (eds.). *Human factors in computing systems: CHI '88 Conference Proceedings.* New York: ACM, 1988, 61–65.
27. Porter, M. E. *Competitive advantage: creating and sustaining superior performance.* New York: Free Press, 1985.
28. Cronin, B. The competitive campus: networking and higher education. *Libri,* 39(3), 173–184.
29. Parker, M. M., Benson, R. J. with Trainor, H. E. *Information economics: linking business performance to information technology.* Englewood Cliffs, NJ: Prentice-Hall, 1988.
30. Simon, H. The steam engine and the computer. What makes technology revolutionary? *Educom Bulletin,* Spring 1987, 2–5.
31. Nelson, T. H. Replacing the printed word: a complete literary system. In Lavington, S. H. (ed.). *Information Processing 80 Congress.* Amsterdam: North-Holland Publishing Company, 1980, 1013–1023.
32. Swanson, D. R. A second example of mutually isolated medical literatures related by implicit, unnoticed connections. *Journal of the American Society for Information Science,* 40(6), 1989, 432–435.
33. Davenport, L. and Cronin, B. What does hypertext offer the

information scientist? *Journal of Information Science,* 15(6), 1989, 369–372.
34. Brand, S. *The media lab: inventing the future at MIT.* Harmondsworth, Eng.: Penguin, 1988.
35. Gelerntner, D. The metamorphosis of information management. *Scientific American,* August 1989, 54–61.

4
COMPETITIVE EDGE

Where to Compete

Where do you compete? In a biological sense, by being smart, by being strong, by being attractive (in terms of the criteria of the moment). In a business sense, by being a leader, not a laggard (smart), by being predator rather than prey (strong), by dominating markets (attractive). These areas of competition can be broken into specifics:

- you compete in time
- you compete on cost
- you compete on price
- you compete on product differentiation
- you compete on quality
- you compete on image

What information do you need in order to compete on each of these dimensions? Take cost, for example. Obviously you need to know the cost structure of the industry and how you compare with competitors. What are typical unit costs? Where are cheap sources of raw materials? Where do your competitors source their materials? What are the delivered and installed costs of a substitute product? What are the associated capital costs if the substitute product is to be matched? The information you need to answer these questions will be drawn from a spectrum of in-house experts (accountants, production managers, bench scientists, procurement specialists) and outsiders (sectoral analysts, suppliers, distributors, industry insiders, dealers, ex-employees, consultants), using both publicly available and private sources. Exhibit 4.1 maps the terrain and players.

What can you do about quality, short of industrial espionage? You can *listen* to suppliers, reverse-engineer products, track the trade press to identify state-of-the-art technologies and services, and, most importantly, *talk* to buyers (wholesalers, retailers, final customers). You can also *look,* by visiting trade fairs, competitor plants and specialist demonstrations. As before, your source mix is heterogeneous; formal, informal, eyes, ears, hands.

How do you reverse-engineer an image? What information do you need to compete successfully where the market is dominated by established brands? How do you compete against exclusivity (the Cartier, Gucci, Ferrari or Bollinger *marques*)? Paloma Picasso has entered the fragrance sector: like other vendors, she is selling pheromones (chemical attractants) and she is selling virtual social mobility (the fantasy of participation in the Picasso *milieu).* Like her competitors, she can to some extent ensure success by deploying a team of market researchers, with a battery of market research techniques for in-depth demographic and psychographic modeling. But the real value of the Paloma brand name is exclusivity: she is selling herself (her face and signature dominate the advertisements). A competitor in this case can carry out equally sophisticated consumer research, but must find a name of comparable *cachet* to front the product.

And how do you compete on innovation? By scanning formal sources (technical journals, databases, product announcements), by using futurologists and by tracking the work of those at the research front. A primary formal source is patent literature. Patents and trademarks exist to protect ideas. In a highly competitive industry like pharmaceutics, where innovation tends to drive profitability, knowledge of the prior art is crucially important. The ability to access historic or archival information can thus be as important as the

EXHIBIT 4.1

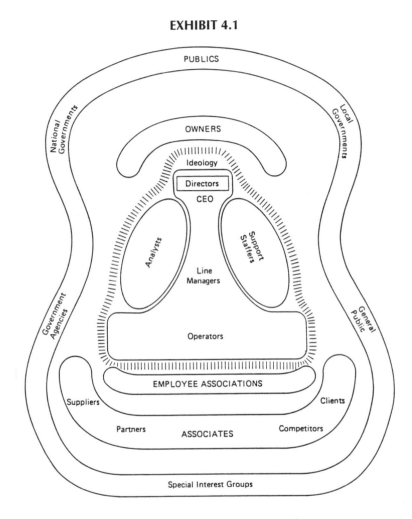

THE ESSENCE OF ORGANIZATIONAL
STRUCTURE

Reprinted with permission of The Free Press, a Division of Macmillan, Inc. from
Mintzberg on management: inside our strange world of organizations, by Henry
Mintzberg.   Copyright © 1989 by Henry Mintzberg.

inputs from industrial "spies." The services of informers (a generic for those who gather informal information) will also be of use; moles, and deep throats who work under cover, or scouts (professional barflies) who gather information by osmosis in public places.

Sources of Advantage

Good coordination is the *sine qua non* of successful competition. Many of our elements of competition will be managed by specialists (accountants know about costs and prices, production managers handle timing and scheduling); their working environment (in terms of structure and technology) must allow them to connect. Generic sources of competitive advantage also include superior strength, nerve and fitness; experience and depth of knowledge; insight into your rival's strengths and weaknesses; inside track on a competitor's intentions; gamesmanship; alliances. These apply as much in business as in sport, or arenas where physical prowess is important.

The athlete's superior strength and fitness translate into manufacturing capacity and reputation, strong market share and cash flow; expertise and depth of knowledge (how to conserve energy; judge conditions) are the equivalents of know-how and proprietary technology; gamesmanship (elbowing or swerving in front of a rival) can be equated with industrial espionage, aggressive advertising ("knocking copy"), or poaching key personnel; alliances (using a pace setter in a middle-distance race; partners in tag wrestling) translate into joint ventures in research and development, marketing, manufacture or distribution, or the creation of a buying group.

Checking the form and track record of a competitor is analogous to carrying out a S.W.O.T. (strengths, weaknesses, opportunities, threats) analysis of industry competitors, while having an inside track on a competitor's intentions (in a take-over bid, for example) means deciphering a barrage of official press releases, company reports and public pronouncements and assessing their reliability. There is, as we said in chapter 2, a difference between public posture and corporate body language: on occasions, the former will be used to conceal actual strategic intentions. Camouflage counts in battle and in business. The role of information technology (heavy artillery, to sustain the military analogy) in leveraging competitive advantage is widely acknowledged: "As labour, in the traditional sense, evaporates in most industries, and capital becomes a globally purchasable commodity, IT will become the tool for building competitive organisational behaviour—along with investments in management. Indeed, the computer industry reflects this with direct labour typically representing only 4% or so of sales."[1]

As we have already said, competitive advantage is achieved on the back of differentiation. A firm can differentiate itself from its rivals using a range of strategies, from reducing costs, through focusing (on a particular market segment), to broadening its scope (offering bundled products or services to its customers). A fuller list is given in exhibit 4.2.

The Oil Mix

Where you are competing on all or many of these fronts, information management is a major issue. In a large multi-national, intelligence may be as strategically important as it is in the military environment. The logistics are similar: coordinating a complex of sources, channels, feeds and outputs; optimizing the technology platform, and using both activities to establish a competitive edge over your adversaries.

In the oil industry, for example, internal information systems are a critical resource as the processes of exploration, extraction, fractionation and distribution depend on detailed and accurate reporting and coordination. Information inten-

EXHIBIT 4.2
Sources of Differentiation

* COST (aim for cost leadership)

* EXCLUSIVITY (superior product quality)

* FOCUS (on a clearly defined market, or market segment)

* SCOPE (offer bundled service/product; vertical integration)

* CUSTOMIZATION (tailor product to expressed market demand)

* DISTRIBUTION (convenience; choice of mode; global reach)

* INNOVATION (stay one step ahead of rivals)

sity is a feature of any company operating in this sector. Competitive edge, therefore, may not depend on external monitoring with a view to knocking out the competition, or securing a geographical niche (unless there is a state monopoly sustained by protectionist legislation), but on prowess in-house (R & D, perfecting a new process, producing a new synthethic material).

It may be linked to quality factors like performing each stage of the production process better, prospecting with fewer misses, extracting with fewer disasters, processing with less pollution, distributing with fewer spills: a strong health and safety record improves street and political credibility. Or (another internal factor) a company may choose to compete on issue management, or the major public concerns of the day (lead pollution; protection of species).

The sector is fiercely competitive and no company can rest on its laurels: since 1980, eleven of the twenty-five US majors have been acquired, merged or sold off. No matter how well a company competes on the factors we have mentioned, forces outside its control can make or break an operation. Oil is a highly volatile commodity, and survival may depend less on cost containment or technological supremacy than on the ability to cope with macro-environmental turbulence (slump in market demand resulting in slashed prices for crude).

In this situation there is a limited number of courses which might put a particular producer at an advantage. A company may choose to enter a cartel, but the advantages here are shared, and may be limited by regulation. What else can a player do? Monitoring of commodity fluctuations can offset the worst of surprises, or a company may choose to lobby at the level of national energy policy (political action committees). Alternatively, producers may choose to invest in macro-level smear campaigns targeted at alternative sources of energy; or they may attempt to boost demand in alternative markets like plastics or animal feeds (diversification strategy).

Whether quality or issue management is the primary focus of competitive activity, detailed and wide-ranging intelligence will be required, what may be called total information, based on systems which can analyze input from wildly disparate sources and global locations. At one end of the spectrum, a company may use lugworms (a common marine species) to detect gas bubbles or leakage; at the other end, expert systems are used as aids to prospecting and fault diagnosis.

Total quality is best assured by integration and interaction. Geographic information systems (GIS), for example, allow major companies to process ever-changing lease maps, to identify optimum locations for gas stations, to create 3-D geological models; these may link with EIS (executive information systems) which can analyze market data, key business indicators, time series data and competitor intelligence (of the non-worm, non-barfly sort). These in turn may integrate with engineering and operations information to ensure that the right spare parts are delivered, or welds accurately performed.

Such capabilities are in place in many companies. Why, in that case, the tanker spillages (Exxon Valdez, Torrey Canyon), the oil platform infernos (Piper Alpha), the refinery explosions (Whiddy Refinery)? Tolerated because infrequent? Or because they don't happen all at once to the same company? Or because intelligence isn't quite total enough? Reports from Piper Alpha that employees reported tell-tale warning signs two days before the disaster suggest that systems are perhaps not optimally participative, or that at the well-head, they are not heeded. Is human resource intelligence all it should be at this level? Do companies know sufficient (in a non-prurient sense) about employee lifestyles, personality traits, skills and motivations for both the company and employees to develop optimally?[2]

A hot issue at the beginning of the nineties is the greening of oil, as much a question of hearts and minds as of health and safety. What sort of intelligence is needed to ensure that *issues* are managed for competitive advantage? The thermoclines of public opinion must be mapped at consumer level; this is as important as tracking and lobbying those who regulate the industry, but, of course, such intelligence may be gathered by competitors. Differentiating the company by acts of philanthropy may be effective: the public may warm to gestures like British Petroleum's endowment of an ecology gallery in the Natural History Museum in London. A detailed knowledge of how consumers' attitudes to issues differ is important. The values which drive environmental concern vary across geographical regions; in the U.K., for example, the Greens worry about health, a sense of duty drives the Germans, the main concern of the Italians is aesthetics. . . .[3] Case presentation and advertising must pick up such nuances. In some cases, however, psychometry is irrelevant; the critical differentiator is location of a gas station, where convenience ensures brand loyalty.

Strategic Information

Competition, then, may be grounded in specifics. In the previous chapter, we explored ways in which the value of information could be quantified in terms of these specifics (time saved; cost reduction). We stressed throughout, however, that many of the benefits of information investment are intangible, and can only be expressed in terms of open-ended variables, like increased market share, whose full value will only be realized after the event. We address such soft variables in this chapter, what might be called the macro elements of competition which affect overall strategy.

The specifics, or micro elements, may be configured to create advantage where it matters most. The *strategic gameboard* [see exhibit 4.3] can focus your thinking. The

EXHIBIT 4.3

The strategic gameboard

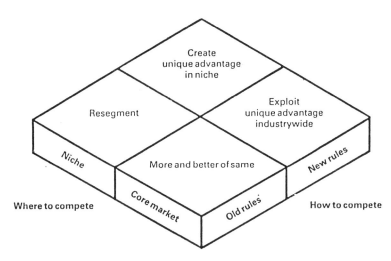

specifics may also be seen as weapons in a war, or pieces in a game. Judicious investment in information and information systems impacts each of these micro elements, but investment, as we have already stressed, will only be effective when linked to business objectives. Given this perspective, the manager's concerns will not be saving dimes and adding bells and whistles, but major issues, like

- the shape of the market
- optimizing intelligence
- competitive posture
- playing the system
- trading risks against rewards.

The Shape of the Market

In economic terms a market is an exchange mechanism, which is shaped by the information available to the participants. In an ideal market, the consumer is assumed to make a rational choice on the basis of perfect information. This, in reality, is impossible to achieve, though some systems approximate to the ideal more closely than others. The types of information which shape perceptions and behavior in markets are what we have labeled the micro elements of competition, cost, differentiation, quality.

Price, for example, is a key determinant of propensity to purchase; in a complex and fractionated market, it is unlikely that the consumer can even approximate to full information. A manager, in contrast, who has greater knowledge of overall price structure than both the consumer and rival producers, may be able to compete effectively on this basis.

A classic example is the use of customer reservation systems in the airline industry, where computerization has produced intense competition on price. In the short run this has benefited the air traveler (predatory pricing resulting in huge discounts; the introduction of frequent flyer schemes), but the pressure on operating costs is such that airlines with tight margins, if not forced to the wall (Braniff, People Express, Laker Airways), will tend to cut back on safety levels (bend or flout Federal Aviation Administration [FAA] rules) and defer investment in replacement planes.

The deregulation of the U.S. airline industry illustrates this scenario: the early euphoria which greeted bargain basement pricing was followed by a wave of discontent with declining service standards, widespread labor unrest, protracted industry restructuring and the emergence of an effective oligarchy.

Optimizing Intelligence

In warfare, intelligence shapes the conduct of battle, and the sum of what is known, or perceived as known, determines the way in which forces are mobilized and deployed. Not always, of course. With better intelligence, we might never have heard of Custer, the Light Brigade or Pearl Harbor. With better intelligence on ISC Technologies, Ferranti International would not have lost $350 million *and* had to sell off its radar business to GEC in 1990. The cost of ignorance (blind spots), whether in war or business, can be spectacular. Lives and careers may be lost.

We have identified a range of techniques and sources which shape the design of competitor intelligence systems (CIS). Such systems, however, are but one facet of an organization's IS (information systems) portfolio. Herein lies the paradox: intelligence shapes business strategy which in turn determines IS investment priorities, yet the funding case for CIS invariably has to be argued along with all other systems proposals.

Intelligence has two main purposes: warning about enemy intentions, and long-term assessment of the enemy's capabilities. The sources of intelligence vary. Some may be covert (and fuel campaigns of subversion or destablization); some may be overt (hard evidence, by direct or remote observation of the adversary's real intentions). Intelligence involves both present perception, and prediction.

Present perceptions may be distorted for a variety of reasons. Preconceptions act as filters of what may be essential information (the "impossibility" of *glasnost* in the U.S.S.R. resulted in disregard of early signs of such a development). Distortion of perception may occur because of what is known as action-reaction interference: "The more absorbed intelligence becomes in understanding the uniqueness of its target, the more it may forget how far the target is responding to its own perceptions of the other side."[4]

In other words, the observer inevitably influences the situation observed. There is a potential dissonance between the intelligence agents and policy-makers; if relations are too distant, the first group will have little credibility in the eyes of the second; if they work too closely together, the second group may bias investigation. Many intelligence operators favor interpretation in terms of worse case scenarios, which may encourage unreasonable pessimism or paranoia. Commercial paranoia, in contrast, may be not only healthy, but necessary (the consequences are less devastating than those of military paranoia).

A crucial component of intelligence is self-awareness or the capacity to see ourselves as others see us, a blind spot in many organizations. Where an enemy's movements are a response to their perception of your own stance, they may take action that is labeled by you "irrational" or "aggressive." In their terms, however, they have made a rational defensive move. In the business field, the capability for self-awareness has been labeled defensive competitor intelligence, that is monitoring and evaluating your business activities as your competitors might perceive them.[5] Routine scanning of standard sources for competitor intelligence on one's own company, and analysis on the same terms as information on rivals, may provide unexpected and important insights.

Self-awareness is now part of standard management training, yet is rarely discussed in the context of business strategy. Exhibit 4.4 is a simple tool which helps to identify blind spots. Where can you get reliable information on how the world sees you, given the prevalence of sycophancy or telling people what they want to hear? Potential sources include press clippings, salesforce gossip, feedback from user groups, customer complaints, employee suggestions, analysts' advice to investors and stockholders, shareholder comments at the company's annual general meetings.

If realistic assessment of the existing competitor environment is difficult, prediction is more so. Past actions may have been intentionally misleading, intended to feed a false profile. Current statements of intent may be equally devious.

The Japanese Way

Japan has had minimal defense obligations since 1945, and the country's resources have been concentrated on commercial, not military, superiority. The Japanese approach to competitors is pragmatic, immediate and grounded in detail; it resembles the body search, rather than large-scale reconnaissance (an analogue of the activity which characterizes many intelligence or long-range planning units in Western corporations, where the military model is considered exemplary). The story of Honda's entry into the U.S. biking sector is one of marketing's classic folk-tales: when their initial model failed (a sure seller in Japan, because its handlebars resembled the eyebrows of the Buddha), the pioneer salesforce camped on the street, and observed the habits and the machines of their clientele . . . the rest is history.

Factory visits and trade fairs are primary hunting grounds, rather than the conference or seminar circuit favored by many marketing units in the U.S. or U.K., and focus on detail is complemented by wide diffusion of observations, with iterative and flexible discussion, role playing and interpretation. Strategy formulation admits many degrees of freedom and multiple perspectives are held to be a source of strength,

EXHIBIT 4.4

JOHARI WINDOW

	Known to self	Unknown to self
Known to others	*Public Arena*	*Blind Spot*
Unknown to others	*Private Life*	*Unknown Area*

4 quadrants ... 4 intelligence objectives

Public arena = optimization
Private life = concealment
Unknown area = penetration
Blind spot = minimization

Reproduced from J. Luft, *Of human interaction*. Palo Alto, CA: Mayfield, 1969. Reprinted by permission of the author.

not confusion. The same questions will be asked over and over again, or with different questioners and respondents to catch every nuance and shift in perspective. These methods harvest information on rivals, and on how other groups see the company (suppliers, or distributors for example).

Social Intelligence

The approaches outlined in this chapter can be also be applied at the level of the state. Take the case of a developing nation, trying to sustain its commodity exports, build up indigenous manufacturing capability, identify alternative sources of energy, or attract foreign direct investment. Where does it turn for reliable information, trend data, intelligence and technological know-how? What kinds of information systems and intelligence effort will be needed?

The problems facing these nations are orders of magnitude greater than those facing industrialized (or newly industrialized) countries. As a bloc, developing countries account for more than 70 percent of world population, 20 percent of trade, 11 percent of industrial production, 7 percent of the global telecommunications infrastructure, less than 6 percent of the world's computers, 5 percent of published scientific output, and 3 percent of R&D expenditures.[6] The gap between first and third worlds can be measured using a variety of indicators such as productivity rates, output levels, capital formation, average income, morbidity and mortality statistics, quality of life factors, and so on. But the divide between the two worlds is also a function of the massive cognitive and social intelligence gaps which exist on almost every conceivable dimension.[7]

At this level, the game is multi-form: it includes aid negotiation, commodity trading, mega-marketing, foreign direct investment, dumping, debt restructuring, price fixing. There is a motley cast of players: transnational corporations (TNCs), non-governmental agencies (NGOs), donor nations, trading partners, creditor banks, lobbyists, peripatetic consultants. The rules are complex, and prone to flux (price taking, debt rescheduling, trans-border data flow, local content levels, nationalization, sequestration). It is a game in which the long-term stakes are high.

Knowledge of the rules and sanctions is important; so too, insights into the strategic thinking and intentions of competitors. In this game, intelligence quality is the difference between losing and losing hopelessly. A panoptic model of a development-orientated intelligence effort is shown in exhibit 4.5. The scope ranges from intelligence on multinationals (track record; intentions; commitment; sensitivity to local

EXHIBIT 4.5

Components of a Development-Orientated Intelligence Effort

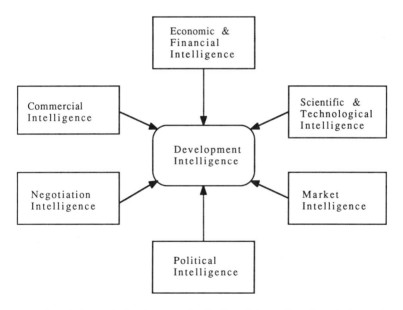

Reproduced from N. Jequier and S. Dedijer, Information, knowledge and intelligence: a general overview. In: S. Dedijer and J. Jequier (eds.), *Intelligence for economic development: an inquiry in the role of the knowledge industry*. Oxford: Berg, 1987, p. 12. Reprinted by permission of the publisher.

conditions; unionization; screwdriver plants or local R&D) through information on science and technology (emergent technologies; "hot spots"; technology licensing opportunities; standards; patenting trends) to market intelligence (shifts in consumer behavior; niche markets; low-cost suppliers).

Systems can be set up to track and store information under each of these headings, but crucial insights or leads will often depend on links being made between disparate elements (the compound value factor we discussed earlier). The results of current research in advanced materials science, for example, should not be stored in a vacuum: new ideas and methods emerging from research laboratories impact on a country's technological and industrial base, and should ultimately translate into marketable products (ranging from consumer goods to the aerospace sector). Intelligence implies connectivity: facts and figures culled from discipline-specific databases should be married to rumors picked up by overseas trade attachés, the results of sectoral studies and other relevant information.

The dice are loaded against third world players, and unless they can change the rules of the game or outflank the competition (powerful and possibly exploitative inward investors), the development gap will widen.[8] How can such countries improve access to knowledge and ideas produced in industrialized nations? How can they hope to penetrate the charmed circle? How can appropriate technologies and processes be identified and successfully transferred? How can home-grown technological capability and skills be fostered and diffused more effectively throughout society? How can indigenous reconnaissance capability be improved?

By changing attitudes. First, government has to recognize that intelligence is "an instrument of development" just as it is an instrument of warfare; second, it must be persuaded of the need for a "development orientated intelligence policy";[9] third, there is a compelling case for reconceptualizing technology transfer as *information* transfer, an idea which the givers of skills and equipment seem to resist; fourth, terrain opacity has to be reduced, if innovations are to spread, information is to be shared and investment encouraged; fifth, government has to realize that strategic information systems planning can contribute to economic development.

Take the last two of these: why have the results of technology transfer so often proved disastrous for the receiver nation? Why so many aborted projects, so many white elephants? One reason is the historic failure to perceive technology as *embodied information,* whose effective transfer depends on the absorption capabilities of the host nation. Technology transfer is a multi-stage, multi-level process of domestication, indigenization and diffusion, in which the quality of information about the technology, its suitability and adaptability, potential and likely secondary local impacts, in addition to intelligence on supplier reliability and motivation, are crucial to smooth transfer.[10]

Secondly, why is it that the great majority of strategic information management systems (SIMS) have been implemented in (a) the private sector and (b) developed economies? By shifting the focus from profit to the promotion of economic health, the fundamentals of SIMS for competitive advantage can be applied in a developing country context. Palvia[11], in fact, has adapted the ideas of Porter and others to construct a conceptual model for SISEDs (strategic information systems for economic development). In addition to the three forces of suppliers, buyers and rivals, government and logistics have been factored into the matrix to take account of third world realities. The result is a set of tools for identifying competitive advantage opportunities, one of which, a scanning grid, is reproduced as exhibit 4.6.

Harvesting Intelligence

How do you harvest intelligence? We list some techniques and sources (formal and informal) in exhibit 4.7. Any of these can be applied to the elements of competition (cost, quality,

EXHIBIT 4.6

Strategic Information Systems for Competitive Advantage
Scanning Grid

– For Developing Countries –

	Suppliers	Customers	Competitors	Government	Logistics
Differentiation					
Cost					
Focus					
Innovation					
Growth					
Alliance					

Reproduced from P. Palvia, S. Palvia, and R. M. Zigli, Models and requirements for using strategic information systems in developing countries. *International Journal of Information Management* 10(2), 1990, 117–126. Reprinted by permission of Butterworth Scientific Ltd.

EXHIBIT 4.7
Intelligence Harvesting

TECHNIQUES	FORMAL SOURCES	INFORMAL SOURCES
Observation	Media	Moles
Eavesdropping	Press (localised)	Scouts/fleas
Reconnaissance	Gov. documents	Journalists
Market research	Speeches	Trade fairs
Reverse engineering	Analysts' reports	PR events
Issue analysis	Patents	Conferences
Planting	Directories	Former employees
Trend analysis	Court records	Old boy network
Empirical testing	Credit information	Dealers/suppliers
Asking questions	Statistics	Customers
Literature search	Consultants	User groups

new products, etc.) to gain specific advantage; combined, they are a strategic information base, which can be tapped and sliced, to profile and project potential competitor behaviors.

A technology platform which supports such activity must be

- flexible
- hospitable
- portable
- distributed
- comfortable

as it must admit input from a cast of players (with disparate experience) dispersed across several stages. Beer[12] has achieved macro-level systems which meet such specifications in Chile and Venezuela [see exhibit 4.8]. These were conceived a decade ago, since when the technology of connective adaptivity has quantum leaped, though costs and unfamiliarity have constrained uptake.

Competitive Posture

The language of posture is important. The Maori war dance performed by the New Zealand All Blacks before their rugby

EXHIBIT 4.8

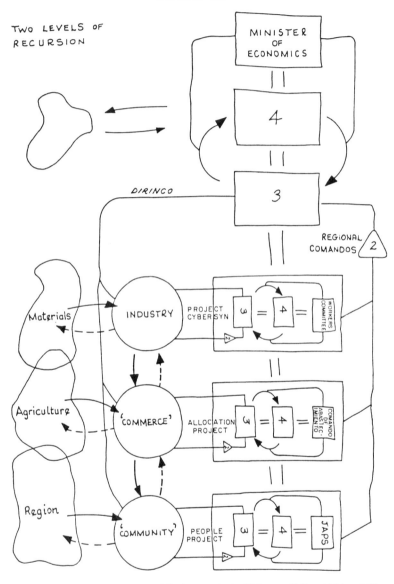

Reproduced from S. Beer, *Brain of the firm,* 2nd ed. Chichester: Wiley, 1981, p. 325.
Reprinted by permission of John Wiley & Sons, Ltd.

matches is designed to unnerve the opposition. Just as animals inflate or raise their hackles, so companies may choose to band together to strengthen their competitive position (the Microelectronics and Computer Technology Corporation [MCC] emerged as a cooperative response to the Japanese Fifth Generation Project). Business also has its overt postures or ritual dances. An illustration of the former is block buying of shares in a target company, a way of unsettling sitting management. Courtship strategies (seeking a white knight in the face of a hostile bid) are a form of ritual dance. An entrepreneur may choose to cast himself as a latter day Napoleon (Robert Maxwell) or find himself cast as a rapacious opportunist (James Goldsmith in his raid on Goodyear). Faced with a predator, a corporation will take every opportunity to portray the bidder as a self-seeking aggressor.

Harder to deal with are hidden hands, games of bluff, political feints: "the grim jockeying for position, the ceaseless trading, the deliberate use of words not for communication but to screen intention. In short, a splendidly exciting game for those who play it." (a paraphrasing of Gore Vidal on politics). This is the world of the casino table: good poker players give nothing away. *They* may be bluffing; *you* cannot be sure. The assets they hold in their hand may be no greater than yours, but their gambling skills give them competitive advantage in tense bidding situations.

Complex business deals have much in common with card games. Hard negotiators are likened to professional poker players, using every piece of information to assess the odds: in a hostile take-over, bargaining positions change as new information is fed into the negotiating process, and as both public and institutional shareholder opinion is manipulated by fresh disclosures (about the raider's downsizing plans or excessive bureaucracy in the target company's HQ).

Roles

Competition implies other players. Except with a monopoly, business presupposes rivalry. The degree of competition will, however, vary enormously: in a mature, consolidated industry, competition between established players may be muted, or sublimated into a cartel (peaceful co-existence). Where a company has a *de facto* monopoly, or an unassailable leadership position, the quest for competition may instead be internalized (like the sprinter who chooses to race against the clock). This can be achieved in one of two ways: (a) by setting (and regularly ratcheting up) exacting quality standards which force company personnel to stay alert and responsive to technological and market changes (a feature of the Japanese consumer goods industry); or (b) by operating an internal market, in which each SBU or LOB competes for central resources.

Each SBU or LOB will consist of individuals who work as a team. On the playing field successful teams rely on impeccable physical coordination and on intimate knowledge of each other's likely initiatives and responses. Knowledge of the opposition may be less intuitive, but nonetheless reasonably detailed (via pre-match analysis sessions).

Your rivals may be of long-standing, or they may be hiding in the wings, unseen or unrecognized as such. Given the volatility of the business environment, roles must not be taken for granted, as the script can change rapidly. It may be imprudent to dismiss potential players on the grounds that they are nominally located in a different business sector: in this jungle, leopards *can* change their spots (AT&T's entry into the computer and information services business is a case in point). Tomorrow's rivals may have little in common with today's. Knowing how to identify new entrants and potential competitors is critically important as a pre-emptive strike may be needed against rivals in search of extra *Lebensraum*.

Reconfiguration of territories may result from political dictat (the formation of a united Europe by 1992; the creation of a value-added network market by means of deregulation).

So scanning of the political environment (infrastructural intelligence) is essential, and knowledge of individual decision-makers (the basis of successful courting strategy) as important as understanding competitors.

Competition occurs at different levels: individual; intra-group; inter-group; international. Alignments and axes are volatile. Individuals compete head-to-head in fencing matches, piano competitions and televised political debate. In business, competition of this kind routinely takes place: between members of the salesforce ("highest over quota"), public service staff ("receptionist of the month"), inventors (numbers of patents logged), and researchers in corporate laboratories (greatest number of discoveries, breakthroughs, patents or publications). There is also intra-organizational competition: in the drug industry it is not uncommon for a number of research divisions or candidate research programs to lobby and compete internally for central funds. In the context of a holding company, each SBU may be treated as an independent profit center and forced to compete against other groups in the portfolio (domestic Darwinism).

But the competition is perhaps most obvious between firms (Redskins vs Bears): slugging it out in the commodity PC market; battling for market share at the luxury end of the automobile market; price discounting in the package holiday industry. And just as we have sporting competitions between nations (the Olympics or World Cup), there is a continuous struggle between nations, whether at the level of a specific commodity (coffee), technology (customized chips), industry sector (biotechnology), or at the level of overall trade (U.S. vs Japan). Competition, of course, can also be analyzed in terms of other economic perspectives, multi-nationals and geo-political blocs.

Rules

Competition usually takes place within a framework of rules. The rules define the parameters of acceptable action (no punching below the belt; bishop moves diagonally) and a serious or persistent breach of a rule may lead to disqualification. Some rules are straightforward and can be divined from observation (quoits); others not (cricket). Many, however, are clearly codified (Queensbury rules; rules of Monopoly™), and such rule sets are the basis of formal business refereeing. In many cases, however, rules are unspoken or opaque, and work as prescriptions for etiquette, which can only be learned by participation in the required social milieu.

In the business context, the appropriate cues can be picked up via surrogates; by observation (who power-breakfasts with whom? what is the correct handshaking/shoulder clasping/ hugging ritual to conclude a deal in a particular culture?) or by consulting published intelligence (trade directories, almanacs, gazetteers, "Who's who's"), but such sources can only offer primary orientation; of more use is conversation with industry insiders (journalists, mentors, consultants, deep throats). Once inside the charmed circle, a player can choose to adopt a low or high profile.

Interpretations of the rules may differ (exactly how and where to replace a golf ball during the course of play; whether to permit use of a dictionary during a formal written examination; the implications of the U.K. Copyright Act for software vendors); or the rules may be inexact (what is the precise definition of insider trading? how should goodwill be valued in accounting terms?), or barely understood (running the bulls of Pamplona). In grey areas, knowledge of precedent or informal norms will be especially valuable.

Ignorance of the law is not be accepted as a defense plea in court, nor will it be in the boardroom. The rules governing the addition of artificial sweeteners to German white wine are clearly laid down. If a spot check reveals excessive saccharine additives, a hefty fine will follow, with the attendant damaging publicity. So too in athletics; anabolic steroids may bring Olympic gold, but the risks are great. If a U.S. computer manufacturer knowingly or unwittingly exports (or facilitates the export of) products (or components) to a "hostile" nation, the consequences can be calamitous, in terms of fines, blacklisting and lost contracts.

Referees

In other cases, the game is transparent: both sides agree to participate according to stated rules. Observance of the rules may be monitored by referees whose remits may include sending players to the sin bin (in ice hockey), sectoral regulation (in financial services we have the Securities and Exchange Commission in the U.S. or the Securities and Investments Board in the U.K.), national anti-trust legislation, inter-governmental or global agreements (the Common Agricultural Policy of the European Community or the General Agreement on Trade and Tariffs). Generally speaking, referees can function in developed and transparent information environments where adequate reporting and enforcement mechanisms can be sustained.

The authority of the referee's decision varies across contexts. Cricket has its umpires whose word is law, but the regulation of American rules football is supported by real-time, slow motion action replay which double checks the human decision. Where wording is ambiguous, or the contexts in which the *ur*-set was conceived have little in common with the prevailing environment, the application of regulations may be hotly disputed (*vide* copyright legislation; *Humanae Vitae*). In such cases, interpretation and arbitration may be necessary, or settlement may be by *fiat* (a high court ruling is laid down; the Pontiff pronounces *ex cathedra*).

Sometimes the rules of the game are set down in a broadbrush manner, with the intention of defining a dynamic, regulatory framework rather than the minutiae of each rule and the detailed conditions under which it might or might not be invoked. This kind of approach has been favored in the telecommunications arena by both the U.S. and U.K. governments in the wake of divestiture and deregulation, with the role of Solomon being played, respectively, by Judge Harold Greene and Professor Bryan Carsberg, backed by the FCC (Federal Communications Commission) and Oftel (Office of Telecommunications). Reading the rules is insufficient in this case: it is necessary to read between the lines and to second guess your competitor's responses to legislators.

Wilmot's following summary of company objectives (italics added) shows how the game metaphor is embedded in the literature of business: "The sense that an organization's key mission is to *compete,* and to *win,* which of course means *beating* someone, is spreading across the entire economy—and is a direct result of *global competition.* No longer is 'better than last year' an acceptable performance. Nor is peddling faster in the same tired and proven way, because *changing the rules of the game* is increasingly the only available route for gaining *competitive advantage. . . . Innovation,* the capacity to do things differently, to change the rules of the game, is a premium. . . ."[13]

Stratagems

Games, as we have pointed out, need rules, players, and in some cases a referee, though this function may be assumed by the participants provided they agree to abide by the rules. In some cases there may be no objective or documented set of rules, and players may not even be aware that they are participating (it doesn't take two to tango). The rules are opaque, and action is defined as a game simply because one player has a set of undivulged strategies to take advantage of the others. Until victims realise they are being taken for a ride, they may unwittingly collude (we looked at this in more detail in the section on social intelligence, where the players are multi-nationals and developing countries).

At what level of complexity and engagement do stratagems become games and games become war? The absence of rules is one feature which distinguishes war (the Geneva Conven-

tion is probably more honored in the breach than observance); this in turn implies a higher degree of complexity, as
rules limit a player's degrees of freedom. The size of the stake
and the scale of participation are other distinguishing
features. War implies loss, devastation, suffering *on both sides,*
and is not undertaken lightly. It may be just, or unjust, but the
cost remains the same. Compulsion is also a feature.
Participants may not have agreed to take part: war is declared,
not negotiated, and often fought by conscripts.

It can be fought on surrogate grounds, psychological,
economic, trade, diplomatic and cultural ("the battle for
hearts and minds"). War is normally overt: tanks roll over
borders; bombs fall from the sky, but you can also have
hidden war conducted through espionage, counter-espionage
and code breaking.

Much of the language of warfare and battle management
has worked its way into the vernacular of business. Companies elaborate defensive strategies (buying back shares),
knock out competitors, battle for and capture market share;
advanced information systems are the basis for launching a
first strike on competitors (ATM technology in banking);
price wars are a regular feature of commodity markets
(pocket calculators, PCs); advertising campaigns are launched
(the Pepsi/Coke ad wars); companies adopt flanking strategies, unveil secret weapons, invade one another's territories,
and occupy niche markets.

The phrase "niche market" is part of another pervasive
metaphor for struggle in the literature of business, ecology.
The Victorian vision of "Nature red in tooth and claw" no
longer holds. Competitors in current terms are simply seen as
"players" seeking a niche in a common territory: their
awareness of rivals, and consequent strategy, need not be
constructed in terms of direct aggression. Strategies for
survival, as we have indicated, may be instinctive or
embodied, rather than calculated. In the animal kingdom,
spots and stripes are not accessories of strife (like warpaint or
camouflage), but in-bred survival and defense mechanisms.

In the case of the manager, this may appear as intuition.[14]

Embodied survival kits will be most effective in a local environment which tends to stability, reinforced by recognized roles and rituals. There are predators and prey, for example, but each knows who the other is, and how they behave. Survival information is acquired by routine and constant scanning: signals are obvious; messages are clear; dirty tricks, black propaganda and misinformation are not required. Evolutionary change is incremental, and paced at a manageable rate.

Business evolution to some extent parallels ecological succession where a maturing environment produces characteristic patterns of consumption (energy inputs, packaged in different forms; what is known as biomass) and diversity (in terms of niches and occupying species). The overall business equivalent of a mature ecology is a well-established marketing environment. The energy or input which drives consumption is information, and diversity appears in a range of products or players or clients. In a mature niche, a long food chain (where a complex and highly developed organism feeds on an organism which feeds on an organism at successively lower levels of development) may be compared to the value chain in a complex organization.

In times of turbulence, generalists (who can tolerate change) or higher-level strategists can survive, but organisms which are over-specialized die out. A similar phenomenon can often be observed in business: "The railroads did not stop growing because the need for passenger and freight transportation declined . . . [t]he reason they defined their industry wrong was because they were railroad-oriented instead of transportation-oriented."[15]

Sizing Up the Odds

Risk involves trade-off: a choice between alternatives. It may be the risk of failing, pure and simple (loss of face or *amour propre*); or the risking of life and limb (ski jumping; pistol dueling), or investment risk (putting your savings into a venture capital company or *premier cru* clarets). How can you hedge against risk? The racing track *habitué* can lay off bets (a form of damage limitation, or risk aversion) while the speculator can hedge by spreading his investments over a range of stocks (from blue chip to high risk). Back-ups and diversification might be business equivalents. Another tactic is to ensure that adequate compensation is paid: ski jumpers would be advised to take out a life insurance policy (though the premium will be prohibitive and in the event of a claim it is the next of kin who will be the beneficiaries); the business analogy might be the penalty clause for non-completion or non-delivery, or the quality guarantee. Or a risk taker can minimize impact: duelists could resort to protective clothing (a bullet-proof vest), through this might increase the risk of loss of reputation.

The risks associated with Formula 1 racing extend beyond the obvious danger to life (the risk faced by the drivers, and to some extent the spectators). Financial risks are taken by the various constructors and backers, as well as the advertisers who lay out millions to have their brand names emblazoned across car bodies and drivers' apparel. The rewards associated with the international *grand prix* circuit are great: so too the risks. However, the cost of entry is prohibitive: in making the decision to compete, consortia have to assess both entry costs (what it takes to assemble and support a traveling circus) and exit barriers (the cost of disassembling or decommissioning a team and disposing of highly specialized plant). The same is true of leading-edge, high-cost information systems investment projects.

Subjective expected utility theory may help you reach an investment decision. Intuitively, we make decisions of this kind every day. On occasion we are more systematic, and identify options on the basis of the probabilities we attach to different outcomes which we fashion into a pay-off matrix. Even fairly systematic probability models, however, are ruffled by surprises. Chaos theory accommodates such perturbations: chaologists have joined the phalanx of analysts available to business strategists.

Risk-taking can be clean (above board) or dirty (of dubious legality). As American as apple pie is the entrepreneur who second-mortgages the family home to generate start-up capital. Less acceptable is the case of the employee with his finger in the pie (insider trading; computer fraud).

People take risks for a variety of reasons. The rewards need not be tangible. Beating the system may be sufficient in itself (the case with most hackers), or the thrill of risk-taking (running a red light). The rewards may be symbolic (a cup, blue riband or plaque), or derive from prestige (claim staking in science; first past the winning post; belle of the ball; *primus inter pares* status). Of course, they may also be monetary. All of these apply in business: improved ROI, profits and stockholder dividends; enlarged remuneration packages and bonuses; cover story status and the hagiography it engenders.

The stakes have escalated in recent years: golden hellos and golden parachutes, stock option schemes and performance-related pay have inflated executive salaries. But as rewards have grown, so too have the risks: hostile raids, greenmailing, LBOs (leveraged buy-outs), downsizing and restructuring have become daily features of corporate life and sharpened the competitive pressures on companies large and small. In the business jungle (to use a hackneyed metaphor) predators and prey need be to alert to all that is going on around them: the quality of an organization's intelligence gathering (the bush telegraph) and analysis capability are increasingly vital to survival.[16]

Tools

What tools are available to make you a better player, a better warrior, or a more skilled survivalist? Porter[17] offers an analytic schema for market reconnoiter or analyzing the competitive structure of any given industry. The five forces (potential entrants, buyer power, supplier power, substitute threat, internal rivalry) shown in exhibit 4.9 are the generic drivers of competition, though their relative influence will vary from industry to industry, and from moment to moment. His model is an all-in-one orientation tool, combining the attributes of a map and compass: it tells you about the lie of the land, your position and direction you are heading. Its utility, however, depends almost wholly on the quality of the information gathered on each of the five dimensions. Although intended as an analytic for use in commercial contexts, the schema can be applied usefully to public sector organizations, provided you make some minor adjustments to the nomenclature.

The model can be used to answer a wide range of strategic questions:

- What are the strengths and weaknesses of the other players in our industry?
- Where are our core LOBs vulnerable, in terms of next generation or successor products?
- Where might potential new entrants emerge from outside the existing set of players?
- What are potential sources of differentiation (new focus, market re-segmentation, predatory pricing, innovation, improved scope)?
- What is known about the structural dynamics of the industry?
- What strategies are likely to yield positive results?

How can Porter's model be linked to the tactics described in this chapter? In a gaming sense, we might want to know what the consequences of moving from one position to another (rook to king four) might be. In manufacturing industry, for example, an option might be forward or backward integration (moving further into territory occupied by an existing supplier of raw materials or upstream into the

EXHIBIT 4.9

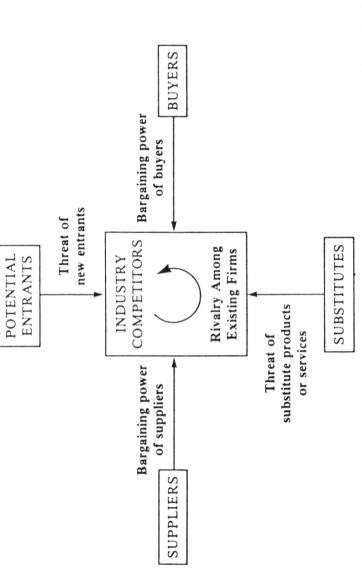

domain of a buyer of semi-processed or finished goods) or strategically relocating a company's headquarter operations.

Blocking strategy (a defensive line-up in gridiron) could be a viable alternative: a company prevents a potential new competitor from moving into the arena by raising the entry level barriers (by upgrading the bedrock technology, thus raising the minimum level of investment required to play the game). A variant on the blocking move might be to form a strategic alliance with other established players (cartelization; joint venturing) to deter would-be interlopers.

Competitive edge can also be gained by changing the pace of the game, an extension of competing in time which forces all players on the field to break new barriers. Some will fail to cope: they will be run off their feet. In industry terms, time ramping may translate into accelerated research or a fore-shortening of the product development cycle.

In terms of warfare, backward integration is the equivalent of securing your supply lines; making sure that the front line troops (in production and processing) have the ammunition and materials to carry on the manufacturing struggle. Forward integration is akin to launching an offensive, seeking to knock out the enemy immediately ahead. Gathering information on the threat of a substitute product and reacting accordingly (upgrading or bundling your existing offerings) is a maneuver to protect your flank. Reconnaissance or scouting in military terms equates with information gathering on potential new entrants.

Porter's model allows you to determine the level of stability within your operating environment (the degree of inter-firm rivalry), and the scope for populating new niches. New entrants may be equated with the arrival of a potentially superior species, or genus, capable of disturbing the prevailing harmony. Links between buyers and suppliers in an industry recall the food chain: one firm feeding off and nurturing another to ensure survival of the system, as we have mentioned. The launch of a radically new product by a major competitor, the introduction of regulatory controls, price discounting or the advent of new players on the scene are the equivalents of turbulence. The result may be that weaker or overspecialized species (companies with lackluster products or narrowly defined markets) may be eliminated.

Portfolio Planning Matrices

The original 2 × 2 portfolio matrix produced by the Boston Consulting Group (BCG) has spawned useful variations, many of which have been reviewed by Ward.[18] The matrix was developed to show how a portfolio of businesses or products might be managed most effectively in a competitive environment. It is now frequently applied in IS/IT assessments within organizations: the matrices show you which way to leap (in terms of product design or information investment).

Organizational information systems can be classified in terms of their strategic significance. Not all are of equal importance: some have tactical, others strategic value. Some have high current utility, others future potential. A second tool is Ward's matrix [see exhibit 4.10] which can be used to group systems into one of four cells, strategic, turnaround, support and factory, in terms of whether their resource consumption (vertical axis) and strategic significance (horizontal axis) are high or low. Calibration and weighting do not feature in this exercise: subjective assessment is all that is required.

The labeling is not definitive: today's factory system may be tomorrow's support system, or last year's problem child (turnaround) may be tomorrow's rising star (strategic). As IS innovations become widely imitated and competitive parity is restored, strategic may be downgraded to factory. In theory, an information system could rotate through each of the four quadrants in the course of its life cycle.

Nor will the classification be the same for all firms in a particular sector; location on the matrix will be a function of

EXHIBIT 4.10

High		
Strategic	Turnaround (or high potential)	
Applications that are critical for future success	Applications that may be of future strategic importance	Strategic impact of future IS
Factory	Support	
Applications that are critical to sustaining existing business	Applications that improve management and performance but are not critical to the business	
Low		

High   Low

Strategic importance of existing operational systems

Reproduced from J. M. Ward, Information systems and technology application portfolio management—an assessment of matrix-based analyses. *Journal of Information Technology*, 3 (3), 1988, 205–214. Reprinted by permission of Chapman & Hall, publishers.

an organization's maturity and its relative systems sophistication. Systems are not in themselves strategic; they acquire the appellation through association. If a business activity is of strategic significance to an organization, the information systems which underpin that function inherit the classification. In another similar company, however, such activities (and the associated systems) might have much lower status.

Ward's matrix relates the value of information systems to both current expenditure and future investment levels. It can be used to review your IS arsenal and to highlight anomalies (where funding is high but IS value is low, or vice versa). It can also be used to plot high- and low-yield information resource entities (where a meaningful distinction can be made between an IS and an IRE).

EXHIBIT 4.11

Degree of interest in information,
Relative market share. Rate of feedback.

	High	Low
Interest in external matters, market growth rate. Risk-taking	**B** Intense interest in information Revival phase Bet your company culture 'STAR' product	**A** Casual attitude to information Development phase Tough guy/macho culture 'QUESTION MARK' products
	C Stable interest in information Maturity phase Work hard/play hard culture 'CASH COW' products	**D** Hostile attitude to information Decline phase Progress culture 'DOGS' products

Reproduced by permission of the Oxford University Press from M. Ginman,
Information culture and business performance. Iatul Quarterly, **2** (2), 1988,
93–106.

We conclude with a version of the BCG matrix which links
information intensity/propensity with key competitive variables. Ginman's[19] model based on detailed interviews with
chief executive officers (CEOs) of SMEs (small- and medium-
sized enterprises) and large corporations suggests a link
between information investment and some variables commonly associated with competitive edge [see exhibit 4.11].
Strassmann's caveats[20] on the dangers of facile association
must, however, be remembered.

References

1. Wilmot, R. W. *Organisational issues and I.T.* A management
   briefing prepared from a presentation to the IBM CUA
   Conference, 21 April 1988. London: Oasis, 1988.
2. See: *The Independent,* 28 October 1989 and *Financial Times,* 28
   October 1989.
3. Derived from the RISC International/ACE (Anticipating
   Change in Europe) System.

4. Herman, M. British and American concepts of intelligence: barriers or aids to cooperation? Paper presented at BISA/ISA Conference, 1989.
5. Ohmae, K. *The mind of the strategist: business planning for competitive advantage.* Harmondsworth, Eng.: Penguin, 1982.
6. Jequier, N. and Dedijer, S. Information, knowledge and intelligence: a general overview. In Dedijer, S. and Jequier, N. (eds.). *Intelligence for economic development: an inquiry into the role of the knowledge industry.* Oxford, Eng.: Berg, 1987, 1–23.
7. Cronin, B. Blind spots and opaque terrains. In Cronin, B. and Tudor-Silovic, N. (eds.). *The knowledge industries: levers of economic and social development in the 1990s.* London: Aslib, 1990, 1–3.
8. Salinas, R. Forget the NWICO . . . and start all over again. *Information Development,* 2(3), 1986, 154–158.
9. Jequier and Dedijer, *op. cit.*
10. Onyango, R. The knowledge industries: aid to technological and industrial development in Africa. In Cronin, B. and Tudor-Silovic, N. (eds.). *The knowledge industries: levers of economic and social development in the 1990s.* London: Aslib, 1990, 5–29.
11. Palvia, P., Pava, S. and Zigli, R. M. Models and requirements for using strategic information systems in developing countries. *International Journal of Information Management,* 10(2), 1990, 117–126.
12. Beer, S. *Brain of the firm.* Chichester: Wiley, 1981. 2nd ed.
13. Wilmot, *op. cit.*
14. Agor, W. H. (ed.). *Intuition in organizations: leading and managing productively.* Beverly Hills: Sage, 1989.
15. Levitt, T. Marketing myopia. *Harvard Business Review,* July–August 1960, 45–56.
16. Cronin, B. New horizons for the information profession: strategic intelligence and competitive advantage. In Dyer, H. and Tseng, G. (eds.). *New horizons for the information profession: meeting the challenge of change.* London: Taylor Graham, 1988, 3–22.
17. Porter, M. E. *Competitive strategy: techniques for analyzing industries and competitors.* New York: Free Press, 1980.
18. Ward, J. M. Information systems and technology application portfolio management—an assessment of matrix-based analyses. *Journal of Information Technology,* 3(3), 1988, 205–214.
19. Ginman, M. Information culture and business performance. *Iatul Quarterly,* 2(2), 1988, 93–106.
20. For a discussion of Strassmann's research see: Huggins, T. Bad managers made worse. *Informatics,* July 1984, 18–19.

5
COMMODITIES AND MARKETS

What is a Commodity?

A commodity is something which is bought and sold, directly or indirectly, and assets, value and competition all come together in the information marketplace. The players (producers and consumers) are a heterogeneous group: in some cases a vendor may be a primary producer in another sector (General Motors; Imperial Chemical Industries) who has exploited spin-off opportunities (EDS; AKS). Others (IBM; Microsoft) offer primary products which are information commodities (workstations; software). The commodity offered may be a final good or an intermediate product.

The nature of markets, where exchange takes place, will vary: barter (direct exchange); mediated trade (via a broker or third party); open or closed (free trade versus protectionism); internal (intra-organizational); external (inter-organizational); dedicated commodity markets (like a stock exchange or metals market). All of these are relevant to information trading.

Information in this chapter is used in the broadest sense. What is bought and sold may be:

- products (books, journals, software packages and other tangible, discrete items)
- services (online hosts; information consultancy and analysis; libraries)
- quanta (patents; formulas; recipes; designs; trademarks)

- capital goods (computers, their components and peripherals)
- channels (business network, broadcast and cable services)

or combinations of these. Take the case of an online search run on a service like Dialog. The database is a product, the host operates a service; a hit, or relevant extracted item, is a quantum of information; the hardware system which holds the data and ports into a network is a capital good, and the telecommunications link is the channel that brings producer and consumer together. Your bill, as a user of the service, will be based on an amalgam of these elements.

What does an information manager need to know about the market? A fundamental feature is the impact of digitization. The information industry has emerged from a convergence of publishing, office automation and networking, the stables which nurtured today's front runners (companies like Reuters, Dow Jones; IBM, Olivetti; AT&T, Northern Telecom). Survival and growth in these sectors have been premised on electronic storage and processing, which result in multiple formats and faceted exploitation, and allow both producers and consumers to slice data in a bonanza of customized service. In discussion of information, it is difficult to separate carrier (hardware and cable) and content, as many products and services are amalgams.

Turn back to exhibit 1.8 in the first chapter (page 27) to the terrain map of the industry produced by the Information Industry Association (IIA) in the mid-1980s. It is a valuable frame of reference as it corrals elements which might not be recognized by many information professionals as part of their field. The eight segments of the diagram, however, have dated. Convergence and fluctuation place many players in a variety of roles: for example, Robert Maxwell's empire includes database vending, financial data services, journal publishing, software production, news and broadcasting media, and a company like Dun & Bradstreet handles a complex portfolio of networked credit information, printed products, travel and investment analysis data services.

Artificial Markets

A second feature of the market is differential development. The term "information industry" is a construct of relatively recent origin. Many major developments have been engineered rather than shaped by market forces [exhibit 5.1]. This is partly due to historical circumstance (the residue from early subsidies, for example, in the online industry is still a source of imbalance in the current market), and partly due to some characteristics of information itself (its non-exclusivity

EXHIBIT 5.1
Policy Instruments

* Subsidy

* Anti-trust

* Consciousness raising

* Championing

* Training

* Protectionism

* Copyright legislation

means that in some contexts it has to be controlled to function as a market good, by, for example, imposing copyright).

The market has been shaped, as we indicate in the previous chapter, through intervention which controls the movement of players: the deregulation of state monopolized telecommunications in both the U.S. and the U.K. has been carefully phased to protect the interests of new entrants. Regulation in the form of anti-trust legislation was a feature of the equipment market of the 1960s as dominance by IBM was challenged by also-rans. In a more recent example from the U.K., IBM was prevented by the Monopolies and Mergers Commission (MMC) from entering a proposed joint venture with British Telecom.

Subsidy to producers is an established instrument of those who shape the information industry. The motives and justification vary. The U.S. government support of Lockheed (the original parent of the Dialog online service) improved the quality of research at NASA (National Aeronautics and Space Administration), by ensuring rapid access to a comprehensive document base; the producer was able to achieve a critical mass of data, and a status as a brand name in the field: "There is no doubt that considerable learning and testing was afforded them by their having had the opportunity to develop full-scale operational systems."[1] In contrast, the support of Minitel by the French government was as much a piece of social engineering to encourage nationwide dissemination of skills and awareness (telematicization) as a lever for specific product development.

Large-scale subsidy (national, or transnational in the case of the European Community) has been instrumental in shaping global markets. Coordination and investment by government have pushed Japan into a dominant position in carefully chosen areas (integrated circuit development, AI). In the early 1980s Japan's perceived lead in fifth generation technology resulted in counterbalancing programs in the U.S. (MCC), the U.K. (Alvey) and Europe (Esprit, Impact, Fast), designed as much to foster a new way of doing things (cooperation) as to produce champion or flagship products and services. Ironically, a feature of such initiatives has been enhanced government/industry liaison, a critical factor of Japanese success.

How else is the market engineered? By consciousness raising and awareness campaigns, by subsidies to users in the form of micros-in-schools initiatives, or incentives to small businesses who wish to automate; by training grants for students on information technology conversion courses, or by proscribing competitor imports, which could damage an infant product or fledgling industry. However, the last of these may prove short-sighted, as technology is often transferred through judiciously negotiated inward investment.

Natural Markets

It may be argued that market engineering and direct intervention have always been necessary features of an industry which did not have an informed consumer base (the idea that information is a commodity is still disputed in certain circles) or the technology to facet and slice, and meet optimum market demand. What drives an ideal market (one with no interference) is consumer demand, but variations in products or services to satisfy every taste can only flourish (a) where there are enough producers to compete and (b) where buyers have the monetary means to choose between products such that there is some incentive for the producer to risk investment in innovation. In many sectors of the information industry, these conditions are not satisfied.

The technologies which enable specialized provision and customized products have only recently been diffused to both supply and demand sides on a scale that even approximates to natural market conditions. To use an industrial age analogy, digitization has become the means of production, distribution and consumption rolled into one.

In chapter 2 we describe a market as mature where a variety of established producers/suppliers offers differentiated goods and services to a broad base of consumers [see exhibit 5.2] and where this activity is supported by information, in the form of advertising, disinterested advice to consumer groups, or reliable user documentation. At this stage of development, simply remaining in the game requires considerable investment, and marketing expenditures progressively rise as a proportion of total operating costs. Some major players in the information industry have reached this stage of development.

The transformation which has taken place in the last twenty or so years is encapsulated in the recent history of the publishing industry. Publishing has long been seen as a "gentleman's" business, sustaining a large number of players. In the last five years, that pattern has changed irrevocably. The small publishing house has become something of an endangered species, being replaced by international combines and conglomerates. Merger and acquisition activity has

EXHIBIT 5.2

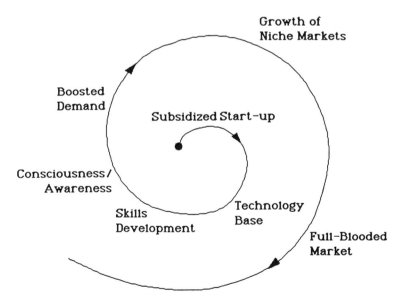

been widespread, with the industry now dominated by a small number of mega-players. Small publishers have been taken over, back lists acquired and artistic criteria edged aside by purely commercial considerations. The industry has been turned on its head.

Tradeable Quanta

Information, packaged as books or reports or journals, has a long history as a marketable product, but publishers on the whole have been slow to recognize information (in the sense of aggregations of quanta which can be reconfigured to suit particular groups) as a commodity, because historically the costs of deconstruction and reconstruction (in terms of fresh typesetting, print runs, and physical reassembly) were high, and adequate sales volume could not be guaranteed. Such economic constraints do not apply in electronic processing, and though publishers appreciate that new technology saves time and money by shortcircuiting some of the *intermediate* stages in the conventional publishing process, they have not recognized the full commercial possibilities of the interim version in the scramble to market a paper-based end-product.

Hardcopy fixes material in a predefined sequence, and it is difficult to assemble material across texts. In contrast, the digitization of the information chain (from collection through organization to distribution) liberates individual items: they can be joined at the consumer's whim in arbitrary order—what is known as on-demand publishing.

With computerized material, individual items of information (like names or addresses) may be shuffled, grouped or processed (according to social class, political coloration, disposable income level, or whatever) to become highly saleable commodities (the backbone of the direct mail advertising industry). Even material which is apparently trivial or transient can furnish a commodity service. Assemblies of news stories culled from newspapers and magazines, and structured according to context, event, product, personality or region, command high premiums in the corporate sector; public domain information, like government trade statistics, when massaged, edited, grouped and displayed as time series data, can be sold to both academic and commercial researchers; jokes overheard in the wash room, or which pop up over and over again on TV programs, or can be found in a compendium on a public library shelf, can be harnessed to create a commercial online database of after dinner stories and witticisms.

The Digitized Market

In chapter 2 we explored the asset potential of government information. Here, we consider in more detail the issues raised by commoditization (equitable pricing and access). The print-based market is well established, and operates through agencies like the GPO (Government Printing Office) or HMSO (Her Majesty's Stationery Office) with public access assured at agreed centers like public/depository libraries and approved retail outlets. In other words: "Information is a commodity which has value, can be bought and sold like any other," to paraphrase a recent U.K. government report.[2] What has been sold? Proceedings, reports, historical analyses, the end results of the processes of government. The electronic market can offer access to the raw material of government, the statistics, the census returns, which can then be analyzed for purposes which lie outside the remit of the state.

Just as iron ore or gold is formed by processes which are independent of the objectives of those who may wish to exploit them commercially, so government information is gathered and stored independently of commercial exploitation. The data are gathered in the course of government by salaried employees, and the costs incurred are not specific to its collection. Those who supply the information (the citizenry, as individuals, as commercial ventures or legal persons) are under obligation; they are not paid, and may be fined if they fail to comply. As no specific cost is attached to supply, or processing and storage, it is difficult to fix a price.

New costing and pricing parameters will apply where raw data are processed, packaged, cut, and distributed in formats which differentiate the product from the basic versions used in government. Here, specific costs *are* incurred, in formatting to suit other systems, indexing for different retrieval software, editing to weed out controversial or sensitive material, reckoning royalties where these apply (crown copyright protects U.K. data). Whether these should be passed on to the consumer may be debated.

A case can be made for recovering full costs (of development and distribution) where a government department or agency sells information generated for its own use, intradepartmentally or to other agencies, on the grounds that the information has been assembled for the making or execution of public policy. As far as the external market is concerned, full cost recovery may be difficult to justify; outsiders may only accept prices which reflect the marginal costs associated with distribution, as they may see full cost recovery as double charging (where the initial gathering has been funded by central taxes). But partial charging is a recipe for market disequilibrium, as it depresses private sector initiative.[3]

In many cases, it may be simpler to contract out. Some departments in the U.K. have already established links with commercial vendors (the Central Statistical Office, which issues trade statistics, for example). In 1986, the Department of Trade and Industry in the U.K. issued a report on Tradeable Information ("data or information in raw or finished form to which the private sector can add value and sell commercially"). The main concerns of a government department, or any organization, which intends to release in-house information to the open market through a third party are outlined[4]:

- extra resourcing in terms of technical support or assistance
- product liability
- ownership of the data (in tape form, for example) and who should retain the primary version
- exploitation of the commercial product by the issuing or originating department (on the basis of some mutually agreed exchange mechanism)
- who is to use the commercial product? (or what is the proposed customer base of the host?)
- do departments want to influence the way the product is marketed?

The report is naive in its assumption that departments can both open their files to third-party development, and retain some degree of control over marketing and clientele, as few entrepreneurs will wish to be inhibited in their choice of clients. The NSA's (National Security Agency's) request to Mead Data Central to divulge the names of its clients accessing NTIS (National Technical Information Service) files was refused. Concern has been expressed that, with privatization, "certain information services and products . . . would not be produced in the market place at all by profit-motivated firms, yet the public desires to have these goods and services." We have used this argument ourselves, in the case of How Britain Votes, a file rescued at the last minute from non-issue by Robert Maxwell.[5] It must be remembered that ideological bias skews the supply side even in the hands of government, as what is selected, processed and distributed is ultimately a political decision. In 1989, the President of the Market Research Society in Britain expressed his concern about "the possibility of information, paid for by the taxpayer, being withheld from the taxpayer —information which on any test ought to be made available for public policy debate."[6]

Distribution mix, in other words, will be influenced by the

political objectives of making information available: those who favor informed participation by citizens will seek to minimize costs and maximize access opportunities. Marketeers, however, will go for profit maximization, a route which may be most easily followed by contracting out responsibilities to third parties. The main questions are:

- should government gather/produce the information itself?
- should it generate the information itself and distribute it through private but subsidized firms?
- should it subsidize recipients (compare foodstamps or education vouchers) but privatize production and distribution?

Government agencies in the U.S. have issued a series of recommendations in this area. The most quoted is OMB A-76: "In the process of governing, the government should not compete with its citizens."[7] Subsequent directives have suggested courting the private sector, by offering inducements (subsidies, tax credits), or permitting the total contracting out of certain services.

Ideology apart (privatization, participation, decentralization), the commoditization of government data offers a niche for small and medium-size companies, where collection and primary processing rest in the hands of government. The high investment costs of locating, formatting and editing a critical mass of data can be avoided, and effects concentrated on market research and customization (two of the companies mentioned in chapter 2, Jordan's and ICC, are major handlers of company filings and credit information in the U.K.; the third, CACI, has processed both U.K. and U.S. census data for over twenty years). Where total privatization is envisaged, the prospect of a Murdoch or a Maxwell controlling major portions of the material of government must raise concern, as does the vision of General Motors, for example, sponsoring information on vehicle licensing or road safety.

Public Goods and Public Good

Libraries are commonly invoked as an example of information as a public good, because they promote literacy, informacy and social interaction. Carnegie's moto "Let there be light" embodies this vision. As with government data, the proposed introduction of charges for this particular public service has generated fierce debate, with polarized positions opposing subsidy and charging, when what is required is a mixed economy[8]: "Tax revenues should be used to subsidize those library services generating external benefits or where the service is seen to be a merit good. But the subsidy is meant to encourage consumption at optimal levels (where the marginal social benefit equals the marginal social cost) and this will usually only require a partial (rather than full) subsidy. The subsidy will be lower where benefits occur in the predominantly private (rather than social) form and, hence, the user charge will be higher. Subsidy and charge are complementary rather than inherently exclusive. Only pure public goods require 100% subsidy on efficiency grounds" [see exhibit 5.3].

There *are* analogies between the consumer of public services and the consumer of private services (of course, there are also differences). A consumer-oriented company will allow a great deal of information to its customers and shareholders (the U.K. paradigm is the Body Shop which has staked its market niche in ecological consciousness), and consumer suggestions will shape both product development and service. A truly consumer-oriented government agency (at local or national level) would similarly allow citizens to shape policy and service, by consulting them throughout the planning process, and ensuring equitable (from all social groupings) representation on working committees.[9]

Such participation would entail an extension of the types of information which are made available to the public. The material which feeds decision making (briefing, background and position papers; forecasts; responses from political action

EXHIBIT 5.3

The differences between private and public goods

	Private good	Public good
1. Exclusion of someone who does not pay	Easy	Difficult
2. Impact of use on supply	Depletes supply	Does not deplete supply
3. Individual's choice of consumption	Choice	No choice
4. Individual's choice of kind and quality of services	Choice	No choice
5. Payment relationship to demand and consumption	Close relationship	Distant relationship
6. Mode of allocation decisions	By market mechanism	By political process

Reproduced from J. L. Crompton and S. Bonk, Pricing objectives for public library services. *Public Library Quarterly*, 2 (1), 1980, 5–22. Reprinted by permission of The Haworth Press, Inc., 10 Alice Street, Binghamton, NY 13904.

committees and other pressure groups) will join data files, or statistical sets. The technology now exists (hypertext, for instance) to analyze decisions in terms of their supporting documentation, and thereby increase the accountability of government.[10] Just what arrangement departments would be willing to make for the distribution of such material is uncertain.

There may be a case for considering government information as an intrinsically imperfect market, which will never shake off the belief of some citizens that "there are certain kinds of entitlement to access to information that should not have the meter running . . . ."[11] Rowe, in an interview for the American Society for Information Science, calls for a new taxonomy, with hot information which is price insensitive (people will pay almost anything) and has a short time frame (it is consumed rapidly), and cold information (which is cheap, stable, underlies the values and infrastructure of the social system and requires subsidy).

There are structural, as well as ideological reasons, for accepting government information as an imperfect market. If a perfect market is one which offers optimum information to consumers, it is clear that government cannot play: it must always exercise a degree of control over what is offered, as many departments are legally constrained in what they can offer on public access (by secrecy and data protection).

Global Markets

We selected globalization as the second fundamental feature of the information industry: many of the principal players operate as transnational companies, and many of the major users of information products and services are themselves multi-nationals. At its most basic, globalization implies trade across national boundaries, which may develop into locally-based manufacturing and R&D facilities (foreign direct investment, as favored by companies like IBM, Mitsubishi,

Ericsson). Products may also be sourced internationally (many of the chips in computing equipment are Japanese) and a company may build an international distribution network or operate through a shipping agent or dealer network (as in the case of software vendors). Each step in this scenario requires the efficient transfer of appropriate information.

This is a prerequisite of global operations in any sector. Like other markets for manufactured goods (cars, televisions), the market for hardware may be disrupted by national interests: machines may be impounded, subjected to fiscal control, banned from entering certain trading areas. The judicious information manager, aware of such factors, will build penalty clauses into contracts for late completion or lack of maintenance.

Such constraints may be difficult to apply, however, in the case of the electronic commodity (data, images, and sound) which is broadcast, wired, microwaved across national boundaries, a problem which preoccupies both national and pan-national legislators, who must adjudicate between players with conflicting interests.

Distributive Justice

Though communication systems facilitate global sweep, they also raise issues which may constrain the effective conduct of business. Where information or data are considered as national property, for example, what should be the span of control of a multinational banking or insurance concern who may wish to process personal name data off-shore? Canada and West Germany are two countries which know the answer: data on nationals must be processed at home; the latter, however, is happy to import data from China, which has shipped data to the West for processing, trading concern about national sovereignty for more pragmatic objectives.

Hegemony may extend beyond information on citizens to

data on land resources, the gene stock (fauna and flora), or the industrial base, which may be all a government has to trade with in the information market, where statistical services are too underdeveloped to act as potential commercial products. The rights issues may be complex: a small, poor country may not have the technology to gather or analyze data on its natural resources, but may assert a moral right to royalties where such data are exploited by outside concerns, rather than acquiescing in the little it has being taken from it.[12]

Satellite transmission can threaten less developed countries in two ways. Some become involuntary exporters (developing countries who cannot afford receivers or processors for remote sensing data). Others are involuntary importers of what they see as cultural contamination. In some states, however, satellite broadcasts may be eagerly embraced, albeit in a black market. In business terms, satellite penetration is important as it allows companies to broaden their advertising base beyond the bounds of conventional display (in the Eastern bloc, for example, where the promotion of consumer goods is heavily underdeveloped). The have-nots of the information world may take their revenge by breaching copyright, trademarks and other protocols which regulate markets in the developed world, and manufacturing and selling counterfeit goods with impunity. Issues of distributive justice are grounded in the distribution of technology, and differential development is as much a cause of exploitation as hegemonic impulses on the part of multi-national corporations. The global information commodity market is predicated on demand for:

- high grade intelligence
- flexible information technology platforms
- universal and reliable distribution channels (e.g., PSS, ISDN)
- cheap, convivial, customized software

Without access to these sources and resources, you cannot play, as we suggest in chapter 3.

Royalties

Information in electronic form has unique characteristics which complicate rewards to producers:

- it is not depletable
- it is non-exclusive
- it can be filtered, compressed, expanded
- it can be deconstructed and reconstructed.

The fact that texts (generically speaking) are not consumed when copies or versions are made allows for a high degree of product differentiation from an original data or textual stock, and many online vendors have found specialist niches in this way. But their non-exclusivity may be a negative factor in pricing; where basic data are offered to a large clientele by a range of vendors, they may have to compete on price, unless, of course, exclusivity is artificially conferred by restricting access or the right to copy. The cost to the buyer of information is an aggregate of the value added at different stages of the production and supply chain. Only a small part of this may attach to the originator of a particular item of information, design, or idea. The rights of such primary producers vary across the five types of commodity, and protection of those rights may be conferred through different legal instruments.

Information products (discrete packages) may be protected by copyright (software has recently been included in this jurisdiction in the U.K.) and so may what we have called quanta, as copyright protects the form or presentation of an idea (as manifest in a design, for example). Many of the components of hardware will be patented, which protects innovation (anything from a circuit board or a proprietary architecture to a keyboard). In both these cases (copyright, patent) the right to exclude others from exploiting the product or invention may be waived on payment of an appropriate fee. Innovative service may also be patented, and franchises granted (McDonalds, The Body Shop). The protection offered to channels is rather different: unauthorized usage is not construed in terms of copying, but in terms of illegal interception. Other legal instruments relevant to the information industry (but not specific to it) are anti-dumping, and anti-trust (which is invoked, inter alia, to prevent cross-subsidy).

What, however, about information services which bundle some, or all of these; a vertically integrated online service, for example? Under recent U.K. legislation, its software (indexing, retrieval, text processing) might be protected under copyright, but the service itself might be construed as cable, with different rights attached.[13] Downloading, which is the *raison d'être* of access in many cases, will or will not be permitted depending on the legal definition of the service.

The law, then, can protect what it recognizes as legally protectable, in terms of recognized crimes (theft, copying and passing off, copying and competing). It cannot protect an idea. Other systems of risk and reward must be invoked; the protocols of scholarship, for example, which recognize priority, or ownership, in terms of first formal publication, and recognize impact, in terms of citation counts and peer esteem. Both have been used to assess the contribution of individuals and institutions to a nation's science base, and to predict productive allocation of government subsidy.[14]

Ideas which emanate from companies are protected by patent and copyright from outside depradation; and employees in many cases accept that innovativeness will be a corporate or team resource, rather than a source of individual kudos. In many successful companies, ideas are deliberately floated in an open (internal) market, by brainstorming, bulletin boarding, collaborative software, as variety and abundance raise corporate IQ. The end product from such an environment which is launched onto the market, and which incurs royalties, may be the result of aggregated effort, but each member of the team foregoes individual rights.

Risks and rewards become more complex in the context of digitized, disaggregated material. Current copyright and theft legislation covers integral or discrete items, not fragments; indeed, fragments may be lifted with impunity from literary works (under fair dealing clauses), as copyright protects the form, not the content. Technologies like hypertext challenge the idea of form where readers (or users) are encouraged to access fragments in a sequence which they find congenial; such form as exists may simply have been suggested by the author as an initial navigational aid, not something which is to be protected.

It is not surprising that rights issues will be handled by contract between producers and publishers and users of electronic material. ADONIS, a joint publishing venture for the dissemination of scientific information on optical media, will operate under licenses which allow users to tailor their reading of the database, select only the pages required, and print in appropriate quantities. The system incorporates an audit process which will allow publishers to tell for the first time exactly what is read.[15]

The situation is further complicated when material is accessed across national boundaries. Take the case of statistics: a researcher may wish to adapt and combine figures which are available from a number of states, not all of which observe the Berne Convention or the Universal Declaration of Copyright: in this example, unilateral rights negotiations may consume valuable time. An added burden may be the negotiation of multimedia rights, to produce sales or training material. An array of agents (Performing Rights Society, for example) must be accessed.

Royalties, in effect, are accrued across a chain of rights which adds costs in the same way as the links in the production chain add value. The manufacturer, however, works to clearly defined parameters; the developer who attempts to compile a marketable commodity from a range of existing electronic products may find that a heavy investment must be made in rights negotiations, and that the process may break down where rights are refused at any point in the chain.

What is required is a unifying mechanism which acknowledges use of material at very small levels of aggregation, and registers payment or appropriate reward at an agreed rate.[16] The system would work across different types of market (commercial, academic, in-house), as it simply involves keeping track across a network, or virtual supply chain. Payment would not be a surrogate for the right to exclude, which would cease to exist and be replaced by a straight accounting mechanism. Usage becomes equivalent to sales.

The market which results will reward high sellers, and value-in-use can be used as a guide to investors, be they government funding bodies, online hosts of full-text, or vendors of value-added network services. Scaremongers who consider such a system vulnerable to payola scandals may ponder the existing best seller domination of book retailing.

Pricing Strategies

We have looked at the shape and growth of the industry (globalization and differential development), and some of the forces which drive exchange (the variety of services and products on offer), the technological driver (digitization), and some of the components of costs (production and rights). But what about price, a key lever of demand in a marketplace? Price is the link between costs (borne by the producer) and value (sought by the consumer), and there are certain generic questions that must be asked in any pricing context:

- what segments of the market are you targeting?
- what is the price range for comparable or competing products?
- what is the pricing history of these rival products?

- what is your benefit segmentation strategy?
- how can you establish and expand market share?
- do you go for immediate revenue generation?

The basis for calculation may be simple (price equals costs plus fixed profit element, what is known as cost-mark-up pricing) or it may be complex (reflecting an array of supply and demand side variables) [see exhibit 5.4]. Pricing may be realistic (demand-oriented), or it may be symbolic. A realistic price will reflect the actual costs of production/delivery and/or intrinsic value of the goods/services to the consumer. Symbolic price is designed to influence consumer perceptions about the product/service on offer: a high price ticket (premium pricing) may suggest exclusivity or superior quality; a low price (loss-leading) may suggest a value-for-money, not-to-be-missed opportunity. Symbolic pricing is used to engineer a market, or position a new product vis-à-vis competitor offerings. Public attitudes and expectations may also influence the range of prices that can be attached to a particular product or service; a six pack of Coke can only retail at a price between $N and $N + n.[17]

Prices will vary between producers and across time: as a function of demand elasticity; in relation to the availability of raw materials, and the costs of production and distribution; in relation to market maturity and product life cycle. Price acts as a signaling mechanism in a marketplace: it sends information to the consumer, but it is also a declaration of intent as far as your competitors are concerned. A sudden drop in price may well be interpreted as a hostile move by a competitor and trigger a price war. In certain cases, price may become *the* most important weapon in a highly contested market.

We look now at pricing as applied to each of the five segments we identified at the beginning of the chapter: information products, services, quanta, capital goods and channels. Of course, elements from this quintet are often bundled, and price structures in the information industry can be enormously heterogeneous.

EXHIBIT 5.4

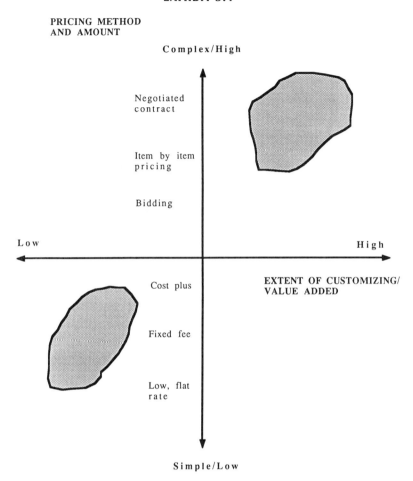

Adapted from A. C. Gross, The information vending machine. *Business Horizons,* Jan.–Feb. 1988, p. 31. Copyright © 1988 by the Foundation for the School of Business at Indiana University. Used with permission.

Products

We start with a familiar product, the print-based publication. Traditionally, this involves a mediated exchange, though some mavericks prefer do-it-yourself dissemination, either because demand is low and the goods would otherwise be unsaleable (vanity publishing), or because the author wishes to retain control. Where mediation entails a number of interventions (keyboarding, editing, mark-up, formatting, typesetting, presentation and packaging, warehousing and distribution, advertising) the publishing process may be seen as a chain, with each link incurring costs which are passed on to the consumer. One way publishers can compete on cost (and thereby price) is to minimize the number of links in the chain by, for example, requiring authors to submit camera-ready copy, or by using desk-top publishing, both of which in effect offload effort from middle man to producer.

Many publishing ventures are spin-offs from organizations where people live by their wits (management consultancies, learned societies, universities, consumer groups). The material is not produced with profit as the primary motive and it may originally have been circulated at subsidized rates on a non-retail basis. Having established a clientele and identified consumer demand, the organization may choose to offer its knowledge stock at the going (or below) market rate, competing directly with mainstream publishers.

The publication of scholarly journals is a highly specialized and peculiar market, which favors the publisher at the expense of both producers and consumers. The raw material is generated at zero cost (academics and researchers *give* their articles to publishers, and in some cases will pay for their papers to appear in print). Not only do publishers have a freely available supply of raw material, but they invariably retain copyright, which facilitates multiple exploitation and repackaging. The end-product is then sold back to the provider community. The economics of scholarly publishing are predicated on (almost guaranteed) demand from the institutional market. Risks are minimal, and costs can be recovered with relatively small print runs. Subscriptions are paid for in advance (thus removing cash flow problems), the consumer purchasing the packaged materials sight unseen. In such cases, the subscription functions as a form of lock-in.

Risks, in contrast, are high in book publishing, where several variables must be considered in estimating a viable print-run, and thereby price. There are production factors to be considered: size and complexity of text (are there graphics? is color required? is an index needed?), rights to be negotiated (advances, royalty agreements, reproduction in alternative media), and consumer demand must be estimated. Publishers in the U.K., however, have been protected against the vagaries of demand by the Net Book Agreement, an anachronistic retail price maintenance mechanism.

The rules of the pricing game are different again in the database arena, which consists of a number of mini markets, distinguished by the consumer's perception of the value of the end-product. The steps in the production process and the attendant costs vary depending on the type of information and the uses to which it will be put. Editing, for example, may involve validation, flagging, normalization; abstracting and indexing are often essential to bibliographic files; specialist software (for data manipulation) may be required; multilinguality may be a necessary feature in certain markets. The same information can be vended in a variety of ways (via print, online, floppy disk, optical media), and the producer may in some cases exploit a cash cow (an established print-based abstracting service, for example) to subsidize the launch of a complementary distribution medium (CD-ROM). Preferential/differential pricing is sometimes used to reduce migration from one product to another (the customer is "rewarded" for his loyalty to the original product) and to sustain a stream of revenue flows.

The marketing of packaged software works in a different way, with versions, or upgrades *replacing* previous products, which have been withdrawn from the market. The customer is effectively locked into a continuous buying cycle, with the attendant hidden cost implications (to operate the software they may have to upgrade their machines and provide additional user training); they will also have to establish who owns the source code. Other features of the software market which affect pricing are site license agreements (equivalent to bulk order discounts), scale economies and built-in protection against piracy and disease (piracy is acknowledged as a cost component, with loss of earnings assumed in the prices set). It is also a market of extremes: established brand names (Lotus, WordPerfect) command customer loyalty, but this will not prevent customers from enjoying and exploiting shareware, packages made available by creative producers at virtually zero cost, the software equivalent of the flea market.

Services

We identified above some of the factors which influence database pricing. With services, other pricing factors need to be taken into account: online prices may reflect a royalty element (paid to the vendor), a computer charge (for cpu time), baud rate differentials, online and off-line record display charges, a telecommunications charge (local call/PSS) and a time-based connection charge. The final price paid by the user will be a combination of these, with variations in how the formula is applied from one service to another. (It may also include an element to cover training and user support.) Many users, however, are unhappy with time-based charges, irrespective of whether the search yields results.

This approach encourages clock watching, and customers are happier with a system based on the number of hits or items extracted: "You have to look at the information that the subscriber is actually getting and build around that as a pricing philosophy."[18] The logic is simple: most users have a search objective, and when that has been satisfied they log off. Time-based charging reeks of behavior modification: stay in the candy store a moment too long and you will be punished. An enlightened retailer will normally be only too pleased to have potential customers on the premises: the facility to browse online is a guarantee of impulse buying.

Such a practice discriminates in particular against those whose queries are open-ended (conducting a literature review; crafting an overview of a topic); less so against those whose search is highly structured or transactional in nature (what is ABC Inc.'s credit rating? how many Fortune 500 companies are headquartered in New York?) In the latter case, the customer can be reasonably sure in advance that the information required will be available and delivered straightforwardly; in the former, the user has no way of knowing exactly what the database contains, how easy it will be to retrieve the relevant information, nor how much time will have to be spend on reformulating the search strategy. With open-ended searches, value-in-use judgments are made after the event. The signs are, however, that discriminatory pricing practices will soon be a thing of the past.

Consultancy is another form of service. We hire consultants to do our thinking for us (or to confirm our own thinking). We are buying ideas, accumulated wisdom, breadth of vision. Traditionally, consultants charge by the hour or day. The price to be paid for services rendered is established at the outset, and the fee handed over on receipt of a satisfactory report. The consumer in this instance has considerable choice: reputation and testimonials can be checked; prices compared. But once the hiring decision is made, expenditure is committed. The consultant's advice is paid for, sight unseen. However, the competitiveness of the market is causing this pattern to change, particularly in the area of strategic information systems consulting, where fees may be results-linked. Here, value-in-use replaces exchange value as the basis of pricing.

The application of pricing to library and information services is confused (many of the policy issues addressed in our discussion of government data apply equally here). In some public sector libraries, charges are levied for selective or expedited services (online searching; in-depth genealogical research; interlibrary loans); alternatively, an annual membership fee may be required. Where services are charged out, there is little evidence of consistent practice, though marginal cost pricing seems to be the favored option. Pricing in this sector tends also to be differentiated (means/status-linked; volume-related), reflecting the variegation of the constituencies being served.

More aggressive pricing may be seen in the private sector. Many industrial information services operate on a charge-back basis, either with the intention of covering costs or generating a profit (you pay the full cost of a market research report or staff time spent on desk research). Their core clients (other departments within the parent organization) are free to use these services, go it alone, or buy in services from outside. This approach goes beyond cost allocation or cost spreading: normal market conditions apply, and there is no *a priori* reason why a successfully managed information service could not offer all or some of its services to external organizations. Effective pricing, however, depends upon knowledge of your customers in terms of their:

- awareness of information value
- propensity to use information
- perception of value-for-money
- availability of alternative sources/suppliers

The approach you take will reflect the information sophistication of your customers at any given moment. Soft (notional) pricing may be necessary to stimulate market interest, to condition your customers and educate them about costs ("if we had charged you, this is what it would look like"); later, hard pricing, based on past usage patterns, is applied. Once the internal market is mature, flexible pricing can be employed as a tool to optimize information resource consumption throughout the organization. This sequence is illustrated in exhibit 5.5 which relates charge-back systems to computer environments.

EXHIBIT 5.5

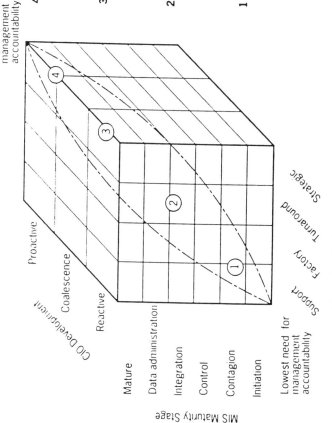

4 Flexible Price Charge Back
   Strategic, mature, proactive.
   Prices set to influence resource
   consumption and maximize benefits
   at low levels of management.

3 Standard Cost Charge Back
   Turnaround, integration, coalescence.
   Future costs are fixed to give users
   more control in budgeting and tracking
   DP expenses.

2 Average Cost Charge Back
   Factory, control, coalescence. Prices
   are based on past usage and costs
   creating fluctuations beyond user
   control. User is charged "hard money."

1 Allocation Charge Back
   Support, initiation, reactive. Prices are
   set to educate high level users about
   DP costs, "soft money" charge.

Reproduced from W. P. McKinnon and E. A. Kallman, Mapping chargeback systems to organizational environments. *MIS Quarterly*, 11 (1), 1987, 13. Reprinted by special permission of the *MIS Quarterly*. Copyright 1987 by the Society for Information Management and the Management Information Systems Research Center at the University of Minnesota.

Quanta

We consider two rather different types of information under the heading of quanta, recipes and patents. What price can be put on a winning recipe, the formula for a successful single malt whiskey, for example? In many cases, such recipes are not patented in order to protect a unique formula; the recipe may be 150 years old, whereas patent protection may not extend beyond twenty years. The mystique which the recipe confers is embodied in brand name, itself a major factor in price setting. Patents, in contrast, are actively traded in the open market. Though they are designed to protect, they are not designed to conceal. The price paid for a patent (or a license to use a patented process) will be a reflection of the buyer's estimation of the long-term impact of the good or service it embodies. In this respect, a patent may be considered a hidden property good.

Capital Goods

The market for equipment is as mixed as the others we have looked at. A variety of exchange relationships exists: at one end of the spectrum a buyer may purchase a commodity PC through a retailer; at the other, the vendor is embedded in the buyer organization, effectively becoming part of the planning team for information investment (what has become known as consultative selling). The exchange between buyer and vendor can be reconstituted as a problem looking for a solution.

The equipment market is complicated by the fact that many purchases are compound, or involve modular acquisition from a number of vendors. In such an environment, compatibility and standardization become important factors in determining consumer choice (not just mips per dollar). How the vendor prices, or differentiates, the product may be immaterial to a buyer who has a particular network configuration in mind. This has transformed the way major vendors sell their equipment; salesmen now present themselves as consultants rather than technicians. Price elasticity, however, is not a feature of the low end of the market (the commodity PC), where predatory pricing is the norm.

Channels

The array of technologies and services currently on offer to the information manager [see exhibit 5.6] affords unprecedented opportunities to develop tailored, highly focused business systems. Increased choice may lead to increased confusion, however, and the information manager must have a clear idea of the technical features offered by each technology and service, and of appropriate market and cost structures. What distinguishes the telecommunications channel market from our four other commodity categories is the tension between public utility objectives and the scope for full-blooded entrepreneurism. It is, in short, another highly individualistic market where idiosyncratic regulatory and tariff mechanisms obtain.

Traditionally, communication channels (telephone, telegraph, telex, broadcast) have been made available through public utilities, working as *de facto* centrally controlled monopolies. This market model was justified because entry costs to the industry were high, and because universal service was a basic objective, at low or uniform cost; this was achieved by public subsidy, cross-subsidy (all received the same service no matter whether they lived in a densely populated area, or rural isolation; in an area with high-volume or low-volume traffic), and advertising support.

The costing model associated with basic service has been undermined by the demand for data communication, by the deregulation of markets to accommodate this demand, and by advances in switching and cable technology which have opened a window for mixed service, and associated differen-

EXHIBIT 5.6

	BASIC	VALUE ADDED

V O I C E	PSTN
	CELLULAR
	BAND III
	SYSTEM 4
	CT2
	MOBILE RADIO
		VOICE MAIL
		VOICE
		   RESPONSE
		VOICE
		   SYNTHESIS

D A T A	PDN PRINET	REAL-TIME DATA EDI MDN
T E X T	FAX TELETEX TELEX	E-MAIL EDI ONLINE INFO SERVICES
I M A G E S	BUSINESS TV	VIDEOCON- FERENCING

Reproduced from F. Gibb and B. Cronin, Networks and competitive advantage. Paper presented at Information Culture et Société: La Montée des Réseaux. Colloque international T.N.S. Université des Sciences Sociales de Grenoble, May 1989.

tial tariffs. Product differentiation is only one factor in the changing cost structure; the shift from labor-intensive to equipment-based service (and the attendant investment implications) is another major variable.

Where customers have a range of services to choose from, pricing will move from being cost-based to value-based. Today's information manager who subscribes to non-basic services will expect to pay more for faster bit streams (T1, T2, DS systems in the U.S. and their equivalents in Europe and elsewhere), enhanced line quality, itemized billing, ISDN (Integrated Services Digital Network) connection, guaranteed service response. Value-based pricing is viable in environments which contrast differentiated and basic service (like the U.K., where a truly competitive environment has yet to emerge). Where full market conditions prevail, with a high degree of *competitive* diversity, producers will be pushed towards cost-based pricing, as is the case in the U.S.

The entrepreneurial opportunities released by recent legislation in the U.K. will affect two main groups of players. Third party vendors of value-added network services (who will mediate between British Telecom and specialized customer groups), and private companies with existing network capability, who may, for example, offer microwave facilities in areas of the country not covered by current providers. Other interested parties are cable TV operators and vendors of mobile communications.

As an alternative to public data services and managed data networks (electronic data interchange, for instance), the information manager might wish to consider data broadcast services which use spare capacity in normal TV transmissions to carry information to specially adapted receivers on a national or regional basis. A single broadcast can reach an unlimited number of users and the unit cost can be extremely competitive; it is a particularly appealing option for distributed organizations, such as retail chains, insurance companies or banks.

Beginner's Guide

In many contexts, of course, information is not a commodity. What we have tried to do in this chapter is outline the conditions which allow it to be treated as one. Where information managers think in terms of markets instead of support or overhead services, they may be better able to clarify their objectives, and improve performance. The provider of an in-house information service, for example, who wishes to sustain company support, may invite his service to be compared with those offered on the open market, and compete on costs (the case we cite in chapter 3 where value is computed as the savings made by not accessing information through a commercial vendor). Alternatively, a manager may wish to enter the open market: we hope that this introduction to its workings and pitfalls may serve as a *vade mecum*.

References

1. Williams, M. E. Information science research, the National Library of Medicine and the public/private sectors. *Online Review,* 6(3), 1982, 253–261.
2. Department of Trade and Industry. *Tradeable information: an introduction.* London: HMSO, 1986.
3. Kent, C. A. The privatizing of government information: economic considerations. *Government Publications Review,* 16 (2), 1989, 113–132.
4. Department of Trade and Industry. *Tradeable information: model contract clauses.* London: HMSO, 1986.
5. Davenport, L. and Cronin, B. Value added reselling and public domain data. *Electronic and Optical Publishing Review,* 7(1), 1987, 8–12.
6. Wass, D. Keynote address to the Market Research Society's Annual Conference in 1989. Quoted in *MRS Newsletter,* April 1989, 48–49.
7. U.S. Office of Management and Budget, *Circular No. A-76,* Section 4.a.
8. Bailey, S. J. Charging for public library services. *Policy and Politics,* 17(1), 1989, 59–74.

9. Pollitt, C. Bringing consumers into performance measurement: concepts, consequences and constraints. *Policy and Politics,* 16(2), 1988, 77–87.

10. Davenport, E. and Cronin, B. *Hypertext and the conduct of science Journal of Documentation,* 46(3), 1990, 175–190.

11. Quoted in: Directions of the information industry. *Bulletin of the American Society for Information Science,* April/May, 1989, 26–28.

12. O'Brien, R. Cruise. *Information economics and power.* London: Hodder and Stoughton, 1983. See also: Smith, A. *The geopolitics of information: how western culture dominates the world.* Oxford: Oxford University Press, 1980.

13. Oppenheim, C. Databases and copyright (Letter to the editor). *Journal of Information Science,* 15(6), 1989, 377–378.

14. Irvine, J. and Martyn, B. R. *Foresight in science: picking the winners.* London: Pinter, 1984.

15. *Information World Review,* February 1990, 18–19.

16. Nelson, T. H. *Literary machines.* San Antonio, TX: The Author, 1987.

17. Arnold, S. E. Stormy weather in the datasphere: the problems of pricing and marketing electronic information. *The Electronic Library,* 7(5), 1989, 309–314.

18. O'Leary, M. Price versus value for online data. *Online,* March 1988, 26–30.

CODA

What do we think we have achieved in these five chapters? Firstly, we persuaded you that information management goes beyond formalism and rigid measurement. Our models and metaphors, and the associated methodologies, are not grounded in mass observation and statistical interpretation. They are intended to illuminate an individual's feel for what is happening, to develop a sense of context which admits a realistic appraisal of opportunities and choices.

Secondly, we hope we have transformed perceptions of the purpose and practice of information management. The changes which result may be major: you may choose to deconstruct an existing service (from monolithic to distributed data processing; from centralized to departmental records management) because you can identify ripple effects across the new configuration. We would hope that the chapter on value might encourage more producers/suppliers to move from a cost-based approach to charging to value-based pricing. Faced with a major IS investment decision, you might base your case on a subjective accounting approach (stressing strategic benefits) rather than conventional cost-benefit analysis. Alternatively, you might have identified areas of opacity in your department or organization; by exploring and adjusting the dominant metaphor(s), you should be able to improve consensus and commitment.

Or the changes may be small scale. You may transform a mailing list (in a learned society or professional organization), an epistolary archive, a database on relocation grants, or a collection of press clippings into a unique product with commercial potential. These local instances are driven by larger *gestalt* changes: the activation of information assets reflects a change in philosophy, from domestic support to active market participation; from auxiliary to entrepreneur.

We have introduced the idea of *total information,* which goes beyond the formal, structured resource described in many information management primers. In addition to persuading you that the informal, the ad hoc, the spontaneous has value, we have brought to your attention techniques and technologies which will help you exploit this cornucopia.

Total information is a powerful change agent which can break down political and conceptual barriers, and dissolve impasses. In this context we raised the issue of distributive justice: if development is construed as information or intelligence, breakthroughs may be possible in the transfer of technology and diffusion of skills. This can happen at the local level, wherever there are pockets of deprivation, or at the global level.

We have emphasized the importance of information as a commodity, but would hope that the limitations of the property metaphor and the problems of maintaining exclusive rights are now clear. Exclusivity is difficult to enforce where information is compiled from fragments, reassembled and distributed on-demand in volatile markets. And we have introduced the notion of a chain of rights which shadows value adding in the delivery/production process.

We believe that intuition is as valuable to management as scientism. The soft models we invoke (from metaphor to matrix) can be used to foster intuition, as they allow you to unravel and control your environment. We hope to have convinced you that they are as important to your professional portfolio as formal models.

BLAISE CRONIN

School of Library and
  Information Science
Indiana University
Bloomington, IN

ELISABETH DAVENPORT

Department of Information
  Science
Strathclyde Business School
University of Strathclyde
Glasgow, Scotland

INDEX